WORK BOOK

the Elect Lady

LIFE'S INTERRUPTIONS
BECOME GODLY OPPORTUNITIES

EDDIE L. LONG

WHITAKER
HOUSE

The Elect Lady Workbook

a study guide companion to *The Elect Lady: Life's Interruptions Become Godly Opportunities*

For speaking engagements, please contact the author at:
New Birth Missionary Baptist Church
P.O. Box 1019
Lithonia, GA 30058
770-696-9600
www.newbirth.org

ISBN: 978-1-60374-024-1
Printed in the United States of America
© 2008 by Eddie L. Long

1030 Hunt Valley Circle
New Kensington, PA 15068
www.whitakerhouse.com

Library of Congress Cataloging-in-Publication Data

Long, Eddie.
The elect lady workbook / Eddie Long.
p.   cm.
Summary: "This study guide companion to *The Elect Lady* helps women find their individual purpose and meaning in God and realize what He can do with a yielded life"—Provided by publisher.
ISBN 978-1-60374-024-1 (trade pbk. : alk. paper) 1. Christian women—Religious life—Textbooks. 2. Submissiveness—Religious aspects—Christianity—Textbooks. 3. Providence and government of God—Textbooks. 4. Control (Psychology)—Religious aspects—Christianity—Textbooks. I. Title.
BV4527.L663 2008
248.8'43—dc22
2007048481

1 2 3 4 5 6 7 8 9 10 11 12 ⨌ 16 15 14 13 12 11 10 09 08

Contents

Introduction 5

How to Use This Study 7

1. To the Elect Lady… 9

2. "If You Leave Me, I Will Die"
   To the Elect Lady… Who Is Our Hero 21

3. Arrested and Interrupted by Destiny
   To the Elect Lady… Whose Plans Have Been Disrupted 31

4. "I Don't Remember the Last Time I Woke Up Happy"
   To the Elect Lady… Who Needs Joy 43

5. Search for Significance in Your Crisis (Never Make It Your Home)
   To the Elect Lady… Who Is Searching for Meaning 55

6. Don't Get Stuck in Transition
   To the Elect Lady… Who Is Caught Up in the Process 67

7. How to Keep Going after Saying "Yes"
   To the Elect Lady… Who Has Agreed to God's Plan 77

8. Don't Reject Your Election
   To the Elect Lady… and Her Acceptance Speech 89

9. Silent Pondering, Public Suffering, Eternal Glory
   To the Elect Lady… and Her Pondering Heart 101

10. From One Elect Lady to Another
    To the Elect Lady… from First Lady Vanessa Long 113

11. "Ain't God Good?"
    To the Elect Lady… and the Encouraging Word 125

12. Preparing the Next Generation of Elect Ones
    To the Elect Lady… Who Is a Sacrificial Nurturer 137

Answer Key 149

About the Author 165

Introduction

The book *The Elect Lady* and this companion study guide were written because I know—on the deepest personal and emotional level—what it is to be raised and "saved" by an Elect Lady. I know what it is to look into loving eyes and say, "You stayed here for me in the midst of your greatest crisis. You are my hero."

I've discovered that God has a special place in His heart for women who sacrifice themselves for others. We see Jesus' own mother elected by God to do an amazing, unprecedented thing—to give birth to God's only begotten Son and to bear the searing pain of watching that same Son die an agonizing death on the cross. I believe that God has a very special name for these ladies—like Mary and so many others—who sacrifice for their children, their spouses, their parents, and the kingdom of God so that His will and love will be expanded throughout the earth. These are Elect Ladies, chosen and anointed to do what few can accept and many do not.

This study is for women in all walks of life, including the Elect Lady and those who have benefited from her love and selfless care. When we look at God's Word, we read a great deal about these remarkable women who give of themselves with a love like Jesus' own. It is a sacrificial love that is difficult, even impossible, to share except for the love of God that is poured into their hearts through God's Holy Spirit. (See Romans 5:5.)

It is my prayer that this study will deepen your understanding of God's special election in your life. I pray that through these pages you will discover the power that will transform your thinking, your relationships, and your life situation. Remember, true success in Christ depends on your ability to trust God with every part of your life.

If you open your heart to the Lord and His Word, I believe that you will be blessed, encouraged, uplifted, and inspired by His precious gemstones of truth. May God's love enfold you as you surrender your heart to His loving will for your life.

In His care,
—*Bishop Eddie L. Long*
Atlanta, Georgia

How to Use This Study

This study guide companion to *The Elect Lady* by Bishop Eddie L. Long is designed for individual or group Bible study. A women's fellowship group or Sunday school class could easily adapt this study into weekly or monthly sessions for discussion and prayer. An answer key is included in the back of the guide for your use.

The study guide consists of twelve chapters. Each chapter review includes the following sections:

Chapter Scripture: These opening verses relate to each chapter topic and can be used for Scripture memorization of God's truth.

Chapter Opening: An introduction of each chapter theme sets the stage for the study questions that follow.

Understanding God's Election: Questions are provided that highlight the truths in each chapter in order to help you understand God's election more clearly. These questions are designed to encourage you to personalize the importance of God's election in your life. Page numbers corresponding to the book are listed for easy reference. Testimony and teaching sections are also included.

Thoughts for Reflection: This is a conclusion to the chapter study and a thought-provoking challenge for you to consider during your personal journal time.

Reflections of the Heart (journal pages): These pages are available for you to record whatever the Lord may reveal to you about your election in God. You can write your disappointments, your joys, and your prayers to the Lord. Open your heart and spirit to hear what God has to say to you in the coming days.

CHAPTER ONE

To the Elect Lady...

"To the elect lady and her children, whom I love in truth, and not only I, but also all those who have known the truth."
—2 John 1:1

For this young lady, everything was fine until her unexpected teen pregnancy. Her fiancé wasn't the father of the child, but he still agreed to marry her in an awkward and early marriage ceremony. Her abrupt disappearance to spend several months with an older relative launched a storm of speculation in her town. Then came her homecoming; obviously she was heavy with child.

After the "hurry-up wedding," this young girl and her husband left for a far village where the baby was born in an emergency "do-it-yourself" delivery. These were the shocking circumstances of her young life, and her neighbors were happy to speculate and gossip about her whenever there was opportunity.

But now, years later, she would read a handwritten letter from someone who was her Son's close associate in His final years on earth. That letter of love began, *"To the **elect** lady..."* (2 John 1:1, emphasis added). Although the letter did not bear her name, she knew John had addressed it to her.[1]

Mary was *elected* or *chosen* for her unique task and mission before the Lord. During this study, you will discover how you were chosen by God for a unique role of *your own* that only *you* can fulfill with His strength and guidance. The Lord will walk beside you every step of the way as you discover the power of His election in your life.

[1.] Some scholars say this letter was written to the church; others believe it was sent to some unknown woman held in high respect long after Mary had died. In my opinion, the epistle of 2 John was addressed to Mary. John's affectionate greeting to *"the elect lady and her children"* is accompanied by a very special closing statement: *"The children of your elect sister greet you"* (v. 13). There is circumstantial evidence that John's mother may have been Salome, sister to Mary. (See Matthew 27:56; Mark 15:40; John 19:25.) This would make John a first cousin to Jesus and would make it very likely that John was writing to Mary, his adopted mother and the birth mother of Jesus.

Notes

UNDERSTANDING GOD'S ELECTION

1. So many others are affected when we are obedient to God and His will for our lives. Mary was elected for a special reason—and so were ordinary people like you and I—to fulfill _____ _____ and to _____ _____ with *eternal* results. (p. 11)

2. According to 1 Corinthians 1:26–29, what has God chosen so that we would not gloat over our own accomplishments, but give Him glory instead? (p. 11)

3. God's calling for your life is based entirely upon _____ and _____ _____, not on your _____ _____ _____. (p. 11)

4. What circumstance has God chosen in your life that seems weak or foolish or difficult to cope with? Is it hard to believe that He will use this circumstance to accomplish His will in your life?

Notes

5. You have the power to accept your election and

_____.

Or you may reject your election and _____

_____. (p. 11)

6. In his second epistle, the apostle John spoke with such love, *"To the elect lady and her children, whom I love..."* Pray right now that the Holy Spirit will move in your heart and let you know how much the Father loves *you* at this moment. Write a few sentences telling the Lord how you feel about the love He has for you.

7. Is it hard to believe God's love? Are you burdened with regrets and questions of "what might have been?" Write down the greatest regret that you might have—a regret that you can then lift to the Lord in prayer. He knows all about those regrets, and He is ready to listen to your heart.

Notes

8. *"To the elect lady..."* Why do these words, written thousands of years ago, trigger such strong reactions in a modern, twenty-first century woman's heart? What hope do they offer? What release can they provide?

9. I am convinced that the force of God's love and election in your life will powerfully break through your regrets and the false face that you show to others. God's love is there to expose _____

_____ , _____

_____ , and _____

_____ we've encountered in life. (p. 13)

10. Have you entertained a direction or a desired destiny you wanted to pursue...until God changed it in some way? What was the direction that you wanted to take?

11. The problem for each of us is the same: we don't choose _____. Destiny _____ . (p. 13)

12. When your dreams for the future seem to be dashed, God speaks a word of great hope to you through the prophet Jeremiah: (p. 14)

"For I know _____
_____*," says the* LORD. *"They are plans* _____
_____ *and not* _____*, to*
give you a _____ *and a*_____*."*

(Jeremiah 29:11–12 NLT)

13. God has some plans for you. They are part of
_____. (p. 14) What are these plans meant to give you? Write it down and then repeat it to yourself. It is God's truth for you!

The apostle John was writing to *the elect lady* but not to a woman who had everything perfect in life. Remember, her life had been *interrupted* by her pregnancy in having her firstborn Son. Surely Mary never expected to conceive before she was married. The Bible says she was a virgin who was *"highly favored"* (Luke 1:28) by God. It was essential for Jesus to have a mother like Mary. She was chosen because she had a heart surrendered to God.

Thirty-three years later, John stood with Mary at the cross while she watched her beloved Son experience an excruciating death. She had the terrible agony of watching Him live a sinless life, but die a sinner's death. How did Mary react to her interrupted life? How will you react to yours?

Notes

Notes

14. In His last moments on the cross, Jesus made two things clear to His mother and to His disciple John. (p. 15)

a. First, _____

_____

_____.

b. Second, _____

_____

_____.

15. Most of us can't stand life's interruptions. Has your life been interrupted by circumstances that you never expected? Do you feel as though your life is "out of control?" (p. 15) Take a few minutes to write down the specific interruptions and prayerfully ask the Lord if these are an election from Him.

16. In 1 Corinthians 10, we are encouraged to remember that whatever our difficulty in life, it will not be more than we can handle. (p. 15)

No test or temptation that comes your way is beyond the course of what others have had to face. All you need to remember is that God _____

_____*; He'll never let you* _____

_____*; He'll always be there to*

_____

_____. *(1 Corinthians 10:13* MSG)

Could there be a more wonderful promise for the elect lady than this?

17. Mary had to deal with several life-changing interruptions in her life, such as her early pregnancy before marriage and the loss of Joseph, making her a young widow. With several sons and daughters to raise, she was also a single mother. Then she watched her eldest Son die, naked, on a cross. (p. 16) Do you have a new concept of Mary today? How are her interruptions in life similar to yours?

18. You have been elected by God to endure some things that other people _____ or_____. (p. 17) Are you still trying to fight for what you want to do instead of accepting what God has for you to do? Write down what you might be doing to prolong the fight.

19. Dear lady, accept God's election now and fulfill His good plans for your life. Your _____ _____ and _____ can be found in only one place—in the position where God elected you to be. (p. 17)

Notes

For years I have experienced the pain of knowing that many wonderful women in my congregation have had major interruptions in their lives. Many of them cry out and pray for mates, helpers, or comforters. These are good prayers, but God may be telling them (and you) that first He wants them to accept God's plan. The Lord may be saying, "If you will accept My plan for you, then I will reveal that I AM is your ever present help in time of need. I know your needs and desires before you even speak them to Me."

20. Look up the following Scriptures and then write them out so that you will remember God's promise to be *all that you need.*

Hebrews 4:16: _____

_____

_____

_____.

Psalm 71:3: _____

_____

_____

_____.

Matthew 6:8: _____

_____

_____

_____.

21. I know that life can be very difficult, but ask yourself honestly, do you have a "poor me" attitude? (p. 19) Do you realize all of the people you can reach with Christ's love no matter what your circumstances? List some of those people who need to be touched by the love of Christ that is in your heart.

22. I believe that the Lord has a word of encouragement for you today, saying, in effect, (pp. 18–19)

    Stop fighting Me, _____. I know you feel your life is ruined because you didn't get _____. You have the power to open your mouth and whisper _____ to man, woman, boy and girl! You can speak the Word of God to so many. Don't lose the opportunity!

23. Elect ladies aren't like other women. What is God doing with the interruptions in their lives? (p. 19)

24. Mary didn't choose her destiny; she _____ to it and _____ it. (p. 20)

25. There are many people who have their lives interrupted by difficult circumstances, but more women's lives seem to be affected than men's lives. Why do you think this is true? You will find some possibilities on page 21, but add a few of your own.

Notes

Notes

_____
_____
_____
_____
_____
_____
_____
_____
_____
_____
_____
_____
_____
_____
_____
_____
_____
_____
_____
_____
_____
_____
_____
_____
_____
_____
_____
_____
_____
_____

26. As difficult as interruptions are, we should understand that our lives are not our own, they have been "_____." (pp. 21–22)

27. Wise parents carefully train their children to _____ _____ and live according _____ while seeking His kingdom _____. (p. 22)

28. Just as my wife Vanessa discovered when we first married, things happen that may dramatically change your life. The way of the Lord may take you _____ _____. (p. 23)

29. Some of the greatest women I've known have had: (p. 25)

a. a deep desire _____ _____;

b. the intellect _____ _____;

c. the personal drive and gifting _____ _____ _____.

30. Again, what has God given you the grace to do? (p. 26)

THOUGHTS FOR REFLECTION

Have you pursued things that God never intended for your life? I believe that all of us have. The crucial problem isn't that you have taken unfortunate detours, but what you will do with those detours now. Will you *get better* or will you *grow bitter*? Will you embrace your election and stand with God and His people, or be like the forgotten fallen who never made it into the Lord's caring church family?

If you've been interrupted on the road to life, and you've found it difficult to recover, I believe that God is saying to you right now, *"To My Elect One, I have given you the grace to do anything you put your heart and mind to in accordance with My good purposes for you."*

Use the Journal in the following pages to record what the Lord has shown you as you search your heart and answer these questions. The Lord will reveal many things to you of His love and His purpose if you will just open your heart to hear Him.

CHAPTER TWO

"If You Leave Me, I Will Die"

To the Elect Lady...
Who Is Our Hero

"Her children rise up and call her blessed."
—Proverbs 31:28

I know—on the deepest personal and emotional level—what it is to point to an Elect Lady and say, "I am here because you were there for me in the midst of your own worst crisis. You stayed when it would have been easier to go. You are my hero."

My hero never finished sixth grade. When her mother got sick, my hero had to leave school and stay home to care for her. Then she married my daddy and became a preacher's wife. Every other year after that, for the next several years, she had a son.

Life with my father wasn't easy. One day, my mother came to grips with her pain and realized that her life was literally messed up. She faced the fact that everything she *had dreamed*, and everything she had ever *hoped for*, just wasn't there. I remember how she cried uncontrollably repeating over and over, "My life is over, my life is over."

On that day, Mom decided to leave. She couldn't stop weeping as she packed her things in her suitcase. Then God interrupted her life. I remember grabbing her in a desperate hug and begging her not to leave: "If you leave me, I will die." I cried as I clung tightly, a little boy who desperately needed his mother.

By God's grace, she heard my plea and stopped packing. I believe that, by her decision, she saved my life that day in countless ways. That day long ago, she set aside her own pain to comfort me, and she never looked back. She stayed and faithfully covered her four sons, even though her circumstances did not improve.

Because my heroic mother denied herself to cover me, I am touching lives all over the world. I find incredible joy in my conviction that God credits Mom's account every time a soul is saved or someone is healed through the ministry He has given me.

UNDERSTANDING GOD'S ELECTION

Notes

1. My heroic mother truly denied herself to cover me. Her willingness to cover me with her motherhood years ago, laid the foundation _____

_____

_____

_____. (pp. 33–34)

2. I sense that my story and that of my mother may be similar to your own story. Who are the Elect Ladies—the heroes—in your life?

3. The day my mother stopped packing and decided to stay I believe she saved my life. Is there a turning point day for you? Can you recall a day when someone changed your life for the better forever?

4. An Elect Lady, like my mother, will remain _____ _____. An Elect Lady will model _____ by being faithful to pay the price. (p. 35)

5. As an Elect Lady, when my mother wanted to run for cover, she held her ground to _____

_____

_____. (p. 35)

Notes

_____
_____
_____
_____
_____
_____
_____
_____
_____
_____
_____
_____
_____
_____
_____
_____
_____
_____
_____
_____
_____
_____
_____
_____
_____
_____
_____
_____
_____
_____
_____
_____
_____
_____
_____

6. Mom sacrificed so much for me. What do you think is the right response to the women (and men) in our lives who have made these kinds of sacrifices? (p. 35)

7. In addition to your answers to question 6, I have two simple answers: (pp. 35–36)

First, _____
_____
_____.

Second, _____
_____
_____.

8. Write down just a few of the many sacrifices that the Elect Ladies in your life made to cover you in your time of need. I believe that the Lord may remind you of some things that time has pushed to the back of your memory.

9. How are you treating those Elect Ladies today? Have you had the opportunity to show them the love and respect that they deserve?

10. Proverbs 31 describes a virtuous woman who is strong and faithful in caring for her family. What response does the Bible say we should have towards those women in Proverbs 31:28? Look up the verse and fill in the blanks.

"Her children _____

_____; her husband*

_____."*

11. Perhaps you are the Elect Lady in the lives of those you love. If they are treating you well, then it is wonderful. If they seem to have forgotten you, you can pray as Jesus did when His sacrifice was being scorned. Look up the verse from Luke 23:34:

"Father, _____

_____."*

12. As in all things, Jesus set *the gold standard* for how to treat His mother. What did He do for her during His time of testing and pain? (p. 36)

13. The Bible is clear how Jesus felt about His mother at the end of His life: (p. 36)

*"When Jesus saw his mother there, and the disciple whom he loved standing nearby, he said to his mother, '*_____

_____' and*

*to the disciple, '*_____

_____.' From that time on, this disciple* _____

_____. Later,*

*knowing that **all was now completed...**"*

(John 19:26–28 NIV, emphasis added)

Notes

14. I believe with all of my heart that the mission isn't complete *until the Elect Lady is covered*. (p. 37) Ask the Lord right now for some specific things you can do to cover the Elect Lady in your own life.

15. If an Elect Lady raises children alone, she must love them, discipline them (which means spanking them when necessary!) and _____ every night. (p. 38)

16. Do you have children, or are you responsible for the care of any children? If so, do you cover those children with your prayers so that they will desire to please the Lord and to accept whatever God has planned for their lives? Please write a prayer here, that *their* dreams will be the same as *God's* dreams for them.

The Bible says in James 5:16, "*The effective, fervent prayer of a righteous man* [or woman] *avails much.*" My brothers and I can tell you that this is very true. My mother prayed for us fervently. In the end, none of us went to jail. None of us ever got in trouble or tried drugs or fathered children out of wedlock.

My mother kept her commitment to us, and now we can keep our commitment to her. Even though she has lost many memories due to progressive dementia, she lives a quiet, happy life in my brother's house in the loving care of his seven daughters, with her other sons, daughters-in-law and grandchildren nearby. God has provided graciously so that we can see to it that she will never lack for anything. She cared for us and covered us until we were grown men, and now it is our turn.

17. I believe that there are many Elect Ladies doing this study right now who can say, as my mother can, "I've walked out my election. In the end I was able to…" (p. 37) Now you complete the sentence with what God has enabled you to accomplish by His grace.

18. Near the end of his life, the apostle Paul spoke about completing his race. Elect Lady, read 2 Timothy 4:7–8 in your Bible and join the apostle Paul as he says:

Notes

I have _____, I have _____, I have _____. Finally, there is laid up for me _____ _____, which the Lord, the righteous Judge, will give to me on that Day, and not to me only but also to all who have loved His appearing.

(2 Timothy 4:7–8)

19. Let's look at Proverbs 31:28 again. What will you rise up and call the Elect Lady in your life?

20. Name at least two women in the Bible (besides Mary) whose lives were interrupted by God—affecting their home, child, or husband. Write them down and consider how the Lord moved in their lives. (See examples in Esther 1v4; 1 Samuel 1–2; Ruth 1–4.)

THOUGHTS FOR REFLECTION

Long ago I cried out in tears and desperation, "If you leave me, I will die." The Elect Lady in my life laid aside her pain, her fears, and her frustration to cover me and preserve my future. You are studying this book because this Elect Lady heard my cry and paid a high price to answer it.

Is someone crying out to you? Has God interrupted your life? How will you answer His summons to destiny? Search your heart for these answers and record them in your journal time.

Notes

Reflections from the Heart

CHAPTER THREE

Arrested and Interrupted by Destiny

To the Elect Lady...

Whose Plans Have Been Disrupted

"Remember, dear brothers and sisters, that few of you were wise in the world's eyes or powerful or wealthy when God called you."

—1 Corinthians 1:26 (NLT)

Rejected. Misunderstood. She was someone more easily disowned than believed. How many Christians in our churches today would have given Mary the benefit of a closer look or a second chance? Would you have been open to the possibility that her story was actually true?

Would we be more interested in pointing out the appearance of sin in Mary's life or in drawing her close to pursue the truth and bring reconciliation? (or restoration if our worst suspicions were true?)

We should be thankful that Joseph was no ordinary man and that he listened and obeyed when God intervened to avert disaster in the nick of time. Sometimes, I wonder if *we* would have done as well as Joseph did that day. Joseph had the faith to believe that God was present and the One who was interrupting Mary's life with His eternal destiny.

Notes

UNDERSTANDING GOD'S ELECTION

1. We always like to know if God is with us in each of our situations. However, _____ _____ are never reliable proofs of God's _____ or _____ in a situation. (p. 42) We know that He is there by faith, because He has promised to never leave us or forsake us. (See Hebrews 14:3.)

2. God was very present in Mary's embarrassing situation, as well as David's life when he was in sin, and Rahab's life, even though she was a harlot. (See 2 Samuel 11 and 12; Joshua 2 and 6.) God does not limit Himself to think the way we think. Write down the words of Almighty God in Isaiah 55:8–9 (KJV): (p. 42)

"For my thoughts _____

_____

_____

_____

_____

_____

_____."

3. Outside circumstances can fool us. Even religious leaders of the day can get so caught up in their own plans that they fail to recognize the hand of God in a situation. What does Paul say in 1 Corinthians 1:25 about the plans of God? (p. 43)

4. How do today's society and Mary's society differ in their reactions to unwed mothers? (p. 43)

5. God elected Mary to do a very difficult thing in this pregnancy. But according to God's plan, Mary had to conceive her child _____

_____

prior to her marriage. (p. 43)

6. God brought Joseph into Mary's situation to give her help and support. Remember, when God elects a woman _____ and places her _____

_____, He will

also _____in the

lives of others who have the power to _____

_____ . (p. 44)

7. In your life, who is the person or persons whom the Lord has provided to support you in your trial or election?

8. We have all experienced situations that would have overwhelmed us if we had known the whole story from the beginning. Since we usually can't handle the full revelation of God's call in our lives, how do we follow His will? (p. 44)

9. The Bible doesn't give us details of Mary's rejection by others. Based on what you know of biblical society, what kind of rejection do you think she probably experienced? (pp. 44–45)

10. Mary submitted to the will of God; name several ways in which she experienced pain from this submission. (p. 45)

11. As the people of God who desire to do the Lord's will, we must never forget that even in the midst of Mary's pain _____

_____

_____.

(p. 46)

12. Simeon delivered a powerful prophecy over Jesus in the temple, yet his word was painful for Mary as well. What was the powerful part of the prophecy for the people of Israel? (pp. 45–46)

13. What was the painful part of Simeon's prophecy for the Elect Lady in Jesus' life? (p. 46)

14. I don't know if Mary ever wondered, *Why me?*, but I think that we all ask that question at some time. If you have been struggling with *why* God has interrupted your life with your circumstances, write your struggle to the Lord right now.

15. We have the ability to choose "the best" life's plan for ourselves. (p. 46)

Circle one:

True or False

Notes

Notes

16. Elect Lady, only God can do the best choosing, and only God can bring to pass His will through your life. Remember what Paul says to us in the first chapter of 1 Corinthians: (p. 46)

Remember, dear brothers and sisters, that few of you were wise in the world's eyes or powerful or wealthy

_____.

Instead, _____

_____ *the world considers foolish in order to shame those who think they are wise. And* _____

_____ *who are powerless to shame those who are powerful.* _____ *despised by the world, things counted as nothing at all, and used them to bring to nothing what the world considers important, so that no one can* _____

_____.

(1 Corinthians 1:26–29 NLT)

17. Don't give up. Surrender to the Lord and His divine destiny. Please, don't surrender to a fateful weakness,

_____

_____. (p. 47)

18. Remember, dear lady, when God intervenes in your life:

a. You've entered _____

_____;

b. The interruption is actually _____

_____;

c. He is _____

to line up with His original plan conceived long before you were born! (p. 47)

19. Why did God elect you to do something that He didn't trust anyone else to do? (p. 47)

20. I know that there are times of unbearable struggle and hopelessness in your life. According to 1 Corinthians 10:13, what promise can you hold on to? (p. 47)

Mary stepped onto a holy roller-coaster ride that brought surprise after surprise to her life. As a pure young maiden, she had dreams of marrying Joseph and raising a family, just like countless young women around her. Mary really didn't know what she was getting into when she told the angel of God, *"Behold the handmaid of the Lord; be it unto me according to thy word"* (Luke 1:38 KJV). She didn't know about the joy and the pain of raising the Son of God to manhood and then watching Him die on the cross. But she had the faith to believe that God would be with her and that He saw her through. Today, she dwells with Jesus in the very presence of the Father.

Elect Lady, surrender to God's will and know that He will stand with you and answer your prayers. Sometimes mothers who have been interrupted by destiny start praying for their prodigal sons and daughters, but they never see the answer to those prayers in their lifetimes. Yet, when those sons and daughters are saved, perhaps those parents or grandparents join with *"so great a cloud of witnesses"* (Hebrews 12:1) to rejoice in heaven.

Notes

_____

_____

_____

_____

_____

_____

_____

_____

_____

_____

_____

_____

_____

_____

_____

_____

_____

_____

_____

_____

_____

_____

_____

_____

_____

_____

_____

_____

_____

_____

_____

_____

21. Our Christian walk really boils down to our trust in God. You must be willing to trust Him with whatever is most precious to you. When does the real challenge of trust come? (p. 50)

22. Thousands of young ladies collide with crushing crisis when they find themselves pregnant and virtually alone. Unlike Mary's circumstances, the Lord did not orchestrate their sin. These hurting young ladies still have the choice of repenting, changing their ways, and going the way of God rather than choosing the _____ _____ and following the

_____

_____. (p. 50)

23. We serve a mighty God who will use even our mistakes for His glory! All life is precious, and before he or she was born, He knew your baby's name and had ____

_____

_____. (p. 50) You do not *ever* have to make the choice to end your baby's life.

24. Please remember that if you or someone you love has had an abortion, there is forgiveness in the Lord. What does the Bible say about sin and our need for cleansing? (p. 51)

25. If there is sin in your life or in the life of someone you love, such as pregnancy before marriage or an abortion, God has freedom for you. Confess _____ _____, ask Him _____ _____, and allow _____ _____ to totally remove your sin and _____ _____. (p. 51)

26. What does 1 John 2:1–2 tell us about sin and who provides our help from sin?

27. You've made mistakes and you may be wondering if God really wants to use you. The answer is _____! God doesn't want His children to sin, but if _____ _____, He can use them to _____. (p. 52)

28. Jesus met with the Samaritan woman at the well and interrupted her life that day. He met her in her sin, disappointments and betrayals. How did Jesus react to her? What did He offer her? What did she become as a result? (pp. 53–54)

Notes

Notes

29. Make your life count! Even if there have been mistakes that seem to overwhelm you, allow Almighty God to turn your life around! (pp. 54–55)

a. Raise the children God gave you _____

_____.

b. Make connections _____,

instead of _____.

c. Make your prison stay _____

_____ and bring God's light _

_____

_____.

30. What will happen if you put God in total control of your life? (p. 55)

THOUGHTS FOR REFLECTION

Pray this prayer with me right now. Today is the day of your salvation. (See 2 Corinthians 6:2.) Don't put it off until it's too late.

Lord, please forgive me for the wrong things I've done and the people I've hurt along the way. I turn away from my old way of life, and I surrender my life to You right now. You arrested me because You love me, and I accept Your election in my life.

Turn my life around right now, in Jesus' name. I trust You with my tomorrow, and I trust You for the strength and ability to do Your will in the days ahead.

Thank You for a fresh start. This moment marks a turnaround, a divine change of direction, in my life. In Jesus' name, amen.

Praise God, your life has just turned around! Worship the Lord in your journal time today!

Notes

"I Don't Remember the Last Time I Woke Up Happy"

To the Elect Lady… Who Needs Joy

"Restore to me the joy of Your salvation, and uphold me by Your generous spirit."
—Psalm 51:12

Any good doctor is careful to prepare patients for the process of healing. If you have surgery, it is normal for your surgeon to warn you about what to expect when you come out of anesthesia, how you are likely to feel, and what to watch out for over the next few weeks.

The same is true when you accept your election by God. Your life will make an instant turnaround in the spirit realm in that moment, but you need to understand how things may go in your daily life when God is at work.

You should have a picture of some of the challenges that may crop up and how they may make you feel. You must be forewarned about what God's Word says concerning key challenges likely to confront you. Why? Satan can always be counted on to try any way possible to kill, steal, or spoil what God is doing in your life! (See John 10:10.) He would like to keep your life joyless. But joy is both a promise and a fruit of the Spirit that Jesus wants you to experience throughout your life.

Notes

UNDERSTANDING GOD'S ELECTION

1. Many people are shocked to learn that what they thought was a very difficult, even a nightmare, existence is actually part of a _____ _____. (p. 58)

2. Can you think of a situation in your life or the life of someone near you that looked so painful but turned out to be a blessing? Explain.

3. Even though Mary's life may have looked like a nightmare to many people, God _____ _____. (p. 59)

4. What did it take from both Mary and Joseph to see God's vision fulfilled through them? How did God lead them for His higher purposes? (p. 59)

5. What were some things about David's situation that made it seem so lowly? (p. 60)

6. David and his whole family discovered that David's nightmare was actually _____ _____ . (p. 60)

7. Even after David's victory over Goliath, when things should have been going better, David was robbed of what four things? (p. 57)

a. _____

b. _____

c. _____

d. _____

_____

8. What did David do when his faith was tested for years with unjust and difficult hardships? (p. 60)

9. During his time of great difficulty, David often cried out to the Lord. You can read his fervent prayers throughout the Psalms. On a 3 x 5 note card, write the words of Psalm 40:1–3 (NASB) below. Read the words of David throughout the day to encourage yourself. God lifted David from the miry clay, and He will do the same for you!

I waited patiently for the LORD; and He inclined to me, and heard my cry. He brought me up out of the pit of destruction, out of the miry clay; and He set my feet upon a rock making my footsteps firm. And He put a new song in my mouth, a song of praise to our God; many will see and fear, and will trust in the LORD.

Psalm 40:1–3 (NASB)

Notes

Notes

10. Can you think of someone who can use this encouragement from Psalm 40:1–3 today? Write their name here, and be certain to share God's Word with them.

11. In the Old Testament book of Ruth, we read about three women who knew what pain and loss were really all about. Naomi lost her _____ and her _____ . Ruth and Orpah lost _____ . (pp. 60–61)

12. The death of Naomi's sons left her totally without support or a home in a foreign land. In biblical times, this would have left her abandoned and without hope. Have you ever felt abandoned and without hope? How did your circumstances compare to Naomi's situation?

You really have to wonder how Naomi and Ruth reacted at first to all of this tragedy in their lives. I wonder if, during those dark days, Naomi ever turned to her daughter-in-law and looked into her tear-stained face to say, "Ruth, can you remember the last time you were happy? Because I can't."

Notes

Elect Lady, how many times have you felt this way, as though you couldn't even remember what it was like to be happy? Do you know that sometimes things get worse before they get better? There are times in our lives when the Lord will allow us to be in extremely difficult situations; He actually turns up the heat in our lives. In the natural world, heat will bring out the impurities in such things as silver, gold, crystals, even steel. It may be working the same way in your life right now to purge the dross—the cares and concerns of this world—and purify your heavenly vision.

God doesn't intend for your life to be unhappy. Joy is one of the fruits of the spirit that God wants to grow in your life. Ruth went on to live a wonderful life in Naomi's homeland. Your life can be transformed as well!

13. Through the difficult times that Ruth experienced, she changed. How was Ruth's heart changed? (p. 62)

14. Ruth spoke some unforgettable words to Naomi that have been used to express devotion and love through the centuries. Let's look at her words recorded in Ruth: (p. 62)

But Ruth said: "_____
_____, or to turn back from following after you; _____
_____, _____;
and wherever you lodge, I will lodge; your people _____
_____, and _____,
_____."   (Ruth 1:16)

Notes

_____
_____
_____
_____
_____
_____
_____
_____
_____
_____
_____
_____
_____
_____
_____
_____
_____
_____
_____
_____
_____
_____
_____
_____
_____
_____
_____
_____
_____
_____
_____

15. For many people, what happened to these women may seem like a nightmare, but it was actually a miracle. What happened when Naomi and Ruth returned to Bethlehem? (p. 63)

16. When God is working in your life, His transforming work in your spirit is instantaneous. The more time-consuming part is the transformation of your

_____, of your _____,

and of your _____ . (p. 64)

17. To be truly transformed by God, how do we need to partner with Him? (p. 64)

18. To obey God means to be open to His will and to die to ourselves. This daily process of personal death and resurrection can produce *pain and discouragement* in our lives. Can you describe a daily process of dying to self that you are going through right now?

Notes

19. Even when we are in the desert season of life with no water in sight, our success depends on our _____ _____. (p. 64)

20. Satan is the enemy of our souls who never wants us to be happy in this life. In the parable of the sower, Jesus explained how Satan schemes day and night to _____ _____ _____. (p. 64)

21. In the parable of the sower, Luke 8:11–15, who does Jesus say comes to take the Word of God out of their hearts? Why does he do it? (p. 65)

22. According to this parable, the devil uses temptation to cause some believers to fall away. How does Satan choke the Word of God? (p. 65)

THE *Elect Lady* WORKBOOK

Notes

If you are struggling to believe God's Word in your situation right now, please look closely at this parable in Luke. Are you being tempted or choked by the things of this world? Is the enemy of your soul using his tactics on you? Write down a tactic that you think is being used against you. Then confess it to someone that you trust who can pray with you against the enemy's wiles. Don't surrender to fatigue or defeat. Perseverance—through faith—is the only way. Stay strong in the Lord and in the power of His might! (See Ephesians 6:10.)

23. No matter what is going on in your life, you can succeed despite obstacles. Jesus is the one who will help you succeed. Look at Jesus' declaration in John 10:10:

"I have come _____

Keep this promise close to you heart, because this abundant life from Jesus will give you the ability to overcome.

24. You must *hear the Word of God* to overcome your difficulties. Name several ways that the Word of God may come to you. (p. 65)

25. To overcome in the Lord, we should hear Him with
a"_____."
This means that your heart is _____
_____
_____. (p. 66)

26. What are some ways that we *keep* the message or the
Word of God? (p. 66)

27. What should our goal in every area of life be? How
should we accomplish all of these things? (p. 66)

28. Do you still feel like saying, "I don't remember the
last time I woke up happy?" Remember, you *can* still see
a harvest in your life *if* _____
_____
_____. (p. 66)

THOUGHTS FOR REFLECTION

Elect Lady, life has been difficult for you. Have you been dealing with depression lately? Have you been sleeping more and yet you're still tired? Do problems overwhelm you more than you can ever remember?

Put your faith and trust in God. He has the power and the will to say, "That day of depression is over!" Even though you might experience temporary dips in your emotional state because of your circumstances, depression is not a place where the born-again Christian has to live! Step into faith with the Lord Jesus Christ. He wants you to experience the power of joy flowing through the darkest passages of your life.

In your journal time, declare to the Lord the hope, faith, love, and joy that you want to have in Him. Read the Psalms and join David in expressing your joy to the Lord. Write out a Psalm that is special to you, or write a "new song" of praise to the Lord from your own heart.

Remember, dear lady, *"This is the day the LORD has made; we will rejoice and be glad in it"* (Psalm 118:24).

Reflections from the Heart

CHAPTER FIVE

Search for Significance in Your Crisis (Never Make It Your Home)

To the Elect Lady…
Who Is Searching for Meaning

"'I know the plans I have for you,' declares the LORD, 'plans for welfare and not for calamity to give you a future and a hope.'"
—*Jeremiah 29:11 (NASB)*

A young boy lies asleep in the darkness and is suddenly awakened by a voice in the quiet of the night. "Samuel! Samuel!" Samuel replies, "Yes, what is it?" running to his master who is asleep in the other room. His master, Eli, looks puzzled and says, "Go back to bed, Samuel. I did not call you." After this occurs two more times, Eli realizes that it is the God of heaven who is calling to young Samuel. But Samuel *"did not yet know the LORD because he had never had a message from the LORD before"* (1 Samuel 3:7 NLT).

I believe that we are like that young boy, Samuel, asleep in spiritual darkness without a clue when suddenly the voice of God will wake us to speak with us. We don't always realize that we are hearing God's voice because we automatically assume He would never speak directly to us. But God does desire to speak to us and wants our ears to be open to His voice.

I also believe that *divine destiny* is buried in the soul of *every* man and woman on earth, whether they call on the name of the Lord or not. A deep longing and desire resonates in each of us—in our inner being—as if a silent voice persistently calls to us, saying, "There is something I have called you to do. There is something I have chosen you to accomplish."

Our place in *God's plan* is what gives us our lives significance.

UNDERSTANDING GOD'S ELECTION

1. Many people have a wrong idea of who God speaks to. They think _____

_____, but no one else does. (p. 70)

2. The truth of the matter is that for Christians, God speaks to each of us, but we don't _____

_____. (p. 70)

3. In the Bible, we see the sins of King David in the Old Testament and the apostle Paul in the New Testament. Because they repented of their sins, God chose to use both David and Paul to help accomplish His purposes. When God chooses to do so, what type of transformed sinners does He use even today? (p. 70)

4. How can we make a difference in people's lives? (p. 71)

5. There is a deeper meaning in life than we usually understand. What is every man and woman looking for in this life? (p. 71)

Notes

Notes

6. Moments of crisis can be significant for many of us because it is the only time that we will discard our

"_____" and seriously

try to define who we are. (p. 71)

7. In our society today (even in the church), most men and women mistake motion and busyness for _____

_____. (p. 71)

8. Name some things that you suspect are just "motions and busyness" in your own personal life.

9. Elect Lady, I know that you are accomplishing many wonderful things in your family and in your church. Please remember that a routine based on _____

_____

_____ is *dramatically* different from a routine _____

_____

_____totally apart _____

_____. (p. 72)

10. I often ask myself, *Where am I and where should I be in God's purposes for my life?* Do you ask yourself the same question? Turn that question into a prayer as you tell the Lord that you desire to be in His will. Record one of those prayers right now.

11. Life is not always as we had planned it. As we each face the reality of that statement, we must also embrace the promise God has for us in Romans 8; (p. 73)

"And we know that _____

_____

_____ *to those who love God, to those who are*

_____

_____."   (Romans 8:28 NASB)

12. We know that God doesn't *send* bad things in our life, but He does _____

_____ because He loves us and has called us for His particular purpose. There is nothing that gives our lives more significance than God's purposes. (p. 73)

    The Lord certainly uses crisis in our lives to help us discover more about who we are and why God elected us. In my life, the crisis of my divorce drove me to the Word and to my knees to search for the significance of my life in Christ. There were days that my failures and circumstances tried to overwhelm me. That is when I learned this vital truth: *You always have a choice in crisis!* We can turn to the Lord as our help and our strength, or we can remain stuck in our crisis and in our pain.

Notes

13. King David was well-acquainted with crisis. In Psalm 23, he describes what the crisis felt like. What did David compare his crisis to in verse 4?

14. We are very familiar with the opening line of Psalm 23: *"The LORD is my shepherd; I shall not want."* What are some of the provisions that David is thanking the Lord for in this Psalm? (p. 73)

a. _____

b. _____

c. _____

d. _____

15. Rather than follow the Shepherd as He walks us through *"the valley of the shadow of death,"* what do we foolishly do instead? (p. 74)

16. Hannah was another Old Testament figure who went through a heart-wrenching crisis. What was her crisis and to whom did she turn in her sorrow? (pp. 74–75)

17. Hannah was an Elect Lady—elected to give birth to the great prophet Samuel. Yet before she had her victory, she had another woman in her life who ridiculed her and accused her of wrong doing. Do you have someone in your life who enjoys seeing your pain? Do you understand the importance of forgiving him or her? Forgiveness brings you *freedom in Christ*. Please write a prayer of forgiveness right now.

18. It is possible for us to become entrapped or stuck in our crisis. If a crisis goes on and on, the worst thing that can happen is when we become _____ _____. (p. 75)

19. The Creator God did not create and save you just so you could tolerate a life of insignificance! What did He call and anoint you to be? (p. 75)

20. The Bible says that we are created to be lifelong victims to our circumstances.

Circle one:

True or **False**

Notes

21. Jesus did not say that He came to bring us lack or difficulties. Again, according to John 10:10, what did He say that He came to bring? (p. 76)

22. In 1 Samuel 1 we see how Hannah turned her crisis into a triumph. How did she do it? (p. 76)

a. She committed _____
_____
_____ .

b. She shared _____
_____
_____ .

23. Whatever your situation in life, _____ is your solution right now! He possesses _____
_____ to
_____ and give you a
_____ ! (p. 77)

24. Now that you have filled in the answers to number 23, I want you to say those words aloud. Say them again! Understand that they are the *absolute truth* for your life. Say them to someone who has been praying for you and stand together on God's promises.

25. If you turn to Jesus with everything in your life, what will He do for you? (p. 77)

26. In Luke 4:18, Jesus shared five crucial reasons why He came to minister on this earth. List them here and remember that they are for you, not just for the people who lived two thousand years ago. The Spirit of the Lord was upon Jesus: (p. 77)

a. He has anointed Me _____

_____;

b. He has sent Me _____

_____,

c. to _____

_____

d. recovery _____

e. to set _____

_____.

27. Jesus has promised release from broken hearts, captivity, and oppression. Anything less than life at this level of freedom is _____!
(p. 77)

28. What should you do when you get sick and tired of your situation? What will God do in response? (p. 77)

Notes

Notes

THOUGHTS FOR REFLECTION

Elect Lady, you have been elected by God to do the impossible. You have been chosen to persevere through things that would have caused other people to surrender in defeat long ago. You are anointed to stand *with dignity* in a place where most people around you would collapse in defeat.

How will you answer these questions of the soul? May the Lord speak to your heart as you spend time in prayer and write in your journal. His will is all the *significance* we need in this life.

a. Did I accept what God told me?

b. Have I stood with Jesus and said, "I am despising the shame of the cross God called me to bear for the joy set before me"? (See Hebrews 12:2.)

c. If there is a greater joy that lies beyond my pain today, then can I capture the joy that lies beyond this task He called me to do?

d. If I have faced the fact that my life is not going the way I wanted it to go, have I finally accepted the direction that God wants me to go?

e. Have I received the joy that God wants to give me when I go in His direction? Have I allowed His joy to become my strength?

CHAPTER SIX

Don't Get Stuck in Transition

To the Elect Lady...
Who Is Caught Up in the Process

*"Let us run with endurance the race that is set before us,
fixing our eyes on Jesus, the author and
perfecter of faith."*
—*Hebrews 12:1–2 (NASB)*

Throughout the Old West, from Kansas to California and from Texas to Oregon, you see the remains of the past if you look hard enough. Old, rusted wagon wheel rims, bleached bones of cattle, remnants of discarded possessions. Thousands of people dared to cross the plains and the mountains of the West in search of gold or land and a new life. Many of them never made it; they died before seeing their desired new homeland, or they turned back because they thought that the road was too hard.

In either situation, they were people who "got stuck in transition" and never reached the other side; they never saw their destinies fulfilled. As children of the Father, we don't have to live our lives stuck in transition!

Notes

UNDERSTANDING GOD'S ELECTION

1. How many times have you blamed yourself for your difficult situation? (p. 80) Write down a decision that you have made that you now regret.

2. Please do not beat yourself up over the decisions you have made that cannot be changed. If you have repented of past sins, they are covered with the blood of Jesus. If you need to repent over past decisions, please ask the Lord for His forgiveness now.

3. What happens when we talk about and keep reliving the mistakes we have made? (p. 80)

4. You don't want to spend your lifetime wringing your hands in despair. Remember the way is _____, _____! (p. 80)

5. Elect Lady of God, your life isn't over! The Lord will get you through this transition. Where should your focus be at this time? (p. 80)

6. If you catch hold _____
_____, you will experience _____
_____ in your
_____, in your _____,
and in the way _____. (p. 81)

7. Do you know how important it is that we talk out loud in order to encourage ourselves in the Lord? You can make statements of truth and encouragement such as: "I will make a mark in the earth that will live from generation to generation." Or, "Because God entrusted me with children, I am _____

_____

_____. (p. 81)

8. Now I would like you to encourage yourself in the Lord with a statement or two that applies directly to your life. God has entrusted you with this election, now write down a statement of encouragement in your situation. Speak that statement aloud everyday for the next week or so until it is really in your heart!

9. What is one of the most discouraging things in life, especially for women? (p. 81)

Notes

_____
_____
_____
_____
_____
_____
_____
_____
_____
_____
_____
_____
_____
_____
_____
_____
_____
_____
_____
_____
_____
_____
_____
_____
_____
_____
_____
_____
_____
_____
_____
_____

10. Many Elect Ladies feel as though they have lost _____
_____, or that they will
never _____
_____. (p. 82)

11. When life is low, God may pick that moment to call
you and remind you that He will enable you to stand
strong in a lifelong _____
_____. (p. 82)

12. What is the most difficult part of a life-long call? In
your own words, describe how you have been dealing
with the call to your election.

13. What can adverse circumstances and unhappy events
push God's elect women to experience? (p. 82)

14. The "Gethsemane experience" is nothing less than a
_____,
a place _____
_____, _____,
and _____. (p. 83)

Many years ago, when I was a newly divorced single parent, the first thing I had to go through was a grieving process. My circumstances forced me to face the reality that life would never be as I had pictured it. My plan was to live my life with my original family in unbroken relationship and in a growing ministry. Divorce changed everything. I recovered from my disappointment because of the Lord's grace and mercy, but I agonized in prayer during the process. However, I didn't get stuck in that process; I moved on to God's victory for my life.

When you reach your Garden of Gethsemane experience, you have a choice to make. "Will I choose to pursue my own will and my preconceived desires for my life? Or, will I say to God, 'Not my will, but Yours, be done'?" Go to the Lord in prayer to recover from your disappointments and to hear His direction and call on your life.

15. It is difficult to be alone during heart-wrenching disappointment or sacrificial decisions. Now is a good time to ask others—people who we know love us and the Lord—to pray with us. Write down the name of one or two people that you believe would listen to your heart and pray with you during this time. Ask them to become your prayer partners during your time of transition.

Notes

16. When God speaks to us, we look for _____ _____ and _____ from the people who are closest and most important to us. We want a word of encouragement that somebody believes in _____ _____. (p. 83)

17. It can be devastating to discover that no one seems to understand what is happening in our lives. Please be careful of those individuals who try to get you to focus on selfish, unbiblical answers to your situation. What types of comments can they make about your husband or children that would tempt you to make the wrong decisions? (p. 84)

18. One trap for folks stuck in transition is to just sit back _____ _____ rather than _____ _____ that they have been elected by God *for a purpose.* (p. 85)

19. Have you ever watched a TV program where everyone (whether informed or not) talked about their interpretation of the significance of life? If you had the opportunity to go on a show such as *Oprah* and state your understanding of life's spiritual significance, what would you say? Write it here.

20. Perhaps God has called you to a sacrifice. It is vital that you understand the *end goal* of the sacrifice in your life. With this understanding comes what kind of joy? (p. 85)

21. Jesus experienced this type of joy in His sacrifice. Look closely at Hebrew 12: (p. 85–86)

> *Let us run with endurance the race that is set before us, fixing our eyes on Jesus, the author and perfecter of faith,*
>
> _____
>
> _____
>
> _____, *and has set down at the right hand of the throne of God.* (Hebrew 12:1–2 NASB)

22. Elect Lady, I have written this study for you and for anyone else who is faced with two all-important decisions. (p. 86)

1. To _____ your life to Christ

   and _____ Him, and

2. to _____ your election to an

   _____.

Notes

23. God wants to work a miracle in your life! With that miracle He also brings a _____ _____. And He promises to _____ _____ _____. (p. 86)

24. The path of "_____" to _____ _____ is the same path that carried Jesus from _____ _____, and beyond the _____ to the right hand of the Father. It is the *right* path for you! (p. 87)

25. If you have already said "yes" to God, you may wonder what this study has for you. Why is it important to continue to look at God's Elect Ladies? What divine appointment could the Lord have for you? (p. 87)

26. Remember, your life _____ _____. You and I have been "_____ _____." We have been set free_____ _____ and bring _____ _____ in His name! (p. 87)

27. God doesn't want us to look *into* heaven; He wants us to look at things *from* heaven. What is the only proper way to see and perceive God's will, especially in the midst of shattered dreams? (p. 88)

28. *What is life all about?* Many people in our culture today are asking themselves this question as they face disappointments in life because they are experiencing real difficulties. What are some of those difficulties? (pp. 90–91)

THOUGHTS FOR REFLECTION

Elect Lady—don't get stuck in transition! God's anointing and provision are upon you—trust Him and stay faithful to His Word one day at a time. Follow the steps that God has given you today and trust Him to continue to lead you tomorrow. You will discover the great things that He has prepared for you. His divine plan is for you to leave a godly mark in the land that will affect generations after you until the Lord returns!

As you turn to your journal time, reflect on all of the things that the Lord has revealed to you so far in this study. Has He spoken to you more clearly about your election that ever before? Write down your heartaches, your questions, and your prayers to Him. He will be there to answer you.

CHAPTER SEVEN

How to Keep Going after Saying "Yes"

To the Elect Lady…
Who Has Agreed to God's Plan

"…and having done everything [that you know to do], *to stand firm."*
—*Ephesians 6:13* (NASB)

Once you say "yes" to God is any area, you will have to say "no" to some of your friends and family and to the critics who refuse to accept your election.

Jesus even had to say "no" to His mother and brothers and neighbors when they failed to perceive a change in His calling and earthly function. (See Matthew 12:16–18.) Jesus was no longer merely the Son who had grown up in Nazareth. The time had come for this Son, whom Mary had covered with her love and her nurturing, to rise up and cover the world on behalf of His heavenly Father.

You may receive criticism from those who misunderstand your election, non-believers and believers alike. Some non-believers may want to see you try to escape your difficult life and take the "easy way" of living in sin. Some believers may misunderstand your election just because you are a woman, or because you have struggled in the past. Stand firm in your decision to accept God's election. Saying "yes" to God will bring with it His direction and His power for all the situations of your life!

Notes

UNDERSTANDING GOD'S ELECTION

1. What is one of the most serious challenges in the body of Christ? (p. 94) What is the empty answer that we dread? (pp. 94–95)

2. When Jesus and the apostles walked the earth, they preached and declared "_____

_____" rather than the local synagogue or the nation of Israel. (p. 95)

3. What are three eternal truths by which every local church should be governed? All of these are based on the eternal Word of God. (p. 95)

4. Write your name in the following blank and then speak these words aloud:

"I, _____, belong to the kingdom of God, so I am a kingdom woman governed by the kingdom principles presented in God's Word. According to Galatians 3:28, *'There is neither male nor female....'*"

5. Genesis 1 tells us that God created the human race male and female. What did He intend for us to do? (p. 96)

6. From the beginning of our species, what did God created men and women to be? (p. 96)

7. Elect Ladies, I thank God for those of you with the courage and character to _____ _____ and raise them in an environment of _____ and _____. (pp. 96–97)

8. There is one Source that provides each of us with the courage and character we need to walk out our election. It is abiding in the vine, and that vine is Jesus Christ. Take a close look at what Jesus said in John 15 about abiding in the Vine: (p. 97)

Abide in Me, and I in you. As the branch cannot bear fruit of itself, _____

_____, so neither can you, _____

_____ _____. I am the vine,

you are the branches; he who abides in Me, and I in him,

_____; for apart

from Me _____.

(John 15:4–5 NASB)

Notes

9. In essence, what is Jesus saying in this passage? When you say "yes" to the election of God, what will He make available to you? (p. 97)

10. Each time we say "yes" to God, another part of our lives comes _____ _____. (p. 97)

11. What has God deposited into your life, and what will that deposit enable you to do? (p. 97)

I am so grateful to God for the treasure that lies within each of us. When we talk about alignment with God, I often think about a safe. We use the dial of a safe to get the alignment right and reach the treasure. The only legitimate way to open a safe is to spin the dial in the right combination of numbers and directions. When we hit it right, something is released and a "tumbler" drops.

It is the same way as we go through the trials and joys of our lives. We experience both difficulties and release. Life takes an unexpected turn and we land in a situation that requires patient persistence until a "tumbler" drops and we are aligned right again. In time, we begin to understand that we are being placed into alignment for a release of God's best in our lives.

The day I grabbed my mother and begged her not to go, a "tumbler" dropped that released God's life-changing grace into my situation. When my school counselor grabbed me in my senior year and spoke to me about my potential and the importance of college, another "tumbler" dropped into the God-ordained combination of my life.

12. Almost immediately after Mary said "yes" to God, life became more difficult. There is a question that we must ask ourselves after we say "yes" to God. How will we keep going? Write your thoughts on this question.

13. Jesus was _____ _____ even though He made all of the right choices and lived a sinless life! His choices (His obedience) didn't allow Him to escape, but they _____ _____ _____ _____. (p. 99)

14. Your obedience to God's election may release into the lives of others: (p. 99)

a. _____

b. _____

c. _____

Notes

Notes

15. Because you are willing to say "yes" to the will of God *today,* what may come to you and your loved ones *tomorrow?* (p. 99)

16. What is the Bible's definition of peace? What is *not* biblical peace? (p. 99)

17. Most of Jesus' disciples were fishermen, so they knew a lot about the winds and the storms that hit the lake called the Sea of Galilee. But they didn't know enough _____. What about your life in the midst of storms? Do you know enough _____? (p. 100) Write your thoughts on how you might know Jesus better.

18. The fourth chapter of Mark describes the storm on the Sea of Galilee that had the disciples so frightened while Jesus slept on the boat. Jesus woke in the storm and simply said "_____!" (Mark 4:39). (p. 100)

19. Jesus and the disciples were already in peace, because the Bible says that Jesus *"is our peace"* in Ephesians 2:14. What did Jesus simply do? What are two characteristics of the peace of God? (p. 100)

20. When the storm rages around us, it is hard to see God's deliverance, but then Jesus says *"Peace, be still,"* and we can _____

_____

_____. (pp. 100–101)

21. Our passage through life is much like the disciples' attempt to cross the Sea of Galilee. Is it hard for you to see God's deliverance in a storm that is rocking you right now? Ask Him for His peace that truly surpasses understanding.

22. Have you wondered whether Jesus cares if you are "drowning" in the difficulties of your life? Are you tempted to believe that your problems are bigger than the God who lives inside of you? Look at the words of the apostle Paul and his solution to your dilemma. (p. 101)

THE *Elect Lady* WORKBOOK

Notes

I don't understand myself at all, for I really want to do what is right, _____. Instead, I do _____.

...It seems to be a fact of life that when _____ _____, I inevitably do what is wrong.

...Who will free me from this life that is dominated by sin?

...Thank God! The answer is _____

_____

....So now there is _____

_____

_____ .

(Romans 7:15, 21, 24–8:1 NLT)

23. Each of us becomes more like Jesus *through a process... with God's help.* (pp. 101–102)

a. _____
b. _____
c. _____
d. _____

24. We would all rather not have the storm but live in the peace of a calm sea. The Lord wants us to learn how to stay at peace even _____ _____. Remember who _____ and understand He is _____ _____. God will never let you _____! (p. 102)

25. In Isaiah 26:3–4, the prophet gives us the secret to enduring peace. Write out his secret in your own words. (p. 102)

26. Elect Lady, how often do you feel alone in your situation, as though no one else could be facing what you must face? When we turn to God's Word again, we find that we *are not* the only one facing our dilemma. (p. 103)

No temptation has overtaken you but _____

_____*; and* _____

_____*, who will* _____

you to be tempted beyond what you are able, but with the

temptation _____

_____*, that you may be able*

_____*.*

(1 Corinthians 10:13 NASB)

27. God will provide you with a way of escape in His timing. When we live in the resurrection power of Jesus Christ, we will not stay down or go under! Something about His presence keeps us afloat in *every* situation. (p. 103) Write a declaration of victory in your own words. "It's going to be tough, but with the Lord's help, I'm going to…

Notes

We may not know the final outcome, but we can know God's peace! Mary's life adventure began the moment she said "yes" to God's election. New chapters of God's mystery in her life unfolded constantly, so she had to live in an attitude of "yes," totally depending on His grace and mercy.

Mary had to give up being the Mary she had dreamed of being most of her young life. God changed her identity with a word. In one brief visitation when Mary said "yes," she went from being a young virgin in her father's house to becoming an outcast among men and the earthly "covering" over the Seed of God, Jesus. When you are not sure what to do in the election of God, you *do the things that you* ***do*** *know to do*. God's mercy, grace and peace will follow.

28. Be careful not to try to fit your election into the accepted group norm. What will the election of God usually do with you and the crowd? (p. 105)

29. Only God's anointing will snap _____

_____

and launch us on a new life of _____

_____! (p. 106)

30. Elect Lady, please remember that once you say "yes" to God's election in your life, you have to _____

_____. You must learn how ___

_____, and your

love _____. (p. 106)

31. Jesus' love for the Father and for us is what enabled Him to minister on this earth and sacrifice Himself on the cross. What did the apostle Paul give up for His love of Jesus the Messiah? (p. 107)

32. Jesus said, *"Whoever desires to come after Me, let him*

_____

_____" (Mark 8:34). When we take up our cross, we lay down our lives in surrender to the One who bring us His resurrection victory!

THOUGHTS FOR REFLECTION

When the election of God grips your heart, His passion isn't far behind. When you finally say "yes," then you've found something and Someone you are willing to risk everything for. Now you can endure the pain, the sacrifice and even the misunderstanding of family and friends, as long as you can see the dream— the One—for whom you are sacrificing.

If you receive the election of God to a difficult task, then He will cause you to believe in and love something so much that you will begin to proclaim your desire to see His will fulfilled in your life. In your journal time, write out your proclamation to the Lord in your own words. (See page 108.) Declare that with God this thing before you *is* possible. Declare your passion for Him and His will above all!

CHAPTER EIGHT

Don't Reject Your Election

To the Elect Lady...
and Her Acceptance Speech

"For it is God who works in you both to will and to do
for His good pleasure."
—*Philippians 2:13*

Sometimes we know what to do but we don't want to do it. When you reject your election, you basically challenge God to change His will for your life. It is better for you to accept the election of God and move forward in the kingdom of God.

I can still remember the night I watched the 2003 gubernatorial election results from the state of California. It made the evening news across the country because, according to the will of the people, the winner was the famous actor, Arnold Schwarzenegger. When he learned that he had won, he stepped before a mass of microphones and made his acceptance speech.

Now I want to ask you, have you surrendered to His will for you? Have you made *your* acceptance speech for God's election in your life? You may be one of the millions of people in this world who is missing the power and authority that God has to offer to those who accept their election. Most of them have missed their opportunities because *they want something else.* Will you let this happen to you?

THE *Elect Lady* WORKBOOK

Notes

UNDERSTANDING GOD'S ELECTION

1. I would like to ask again, *have you made your acceptance speech for your election?* Have you made a statement to the Lord that acknowledges the surrender of your will to His? If you have, record when and where it took place.

2. I believe that people miss the mark with the Lord when they succumb to the "I/O Factor." What is the "I/O Factor"? (p. 111)

3. What can happen if you succumb to the "I/O Factor"?

4. "If only…" are two words that are deadly. They lock you into an eternity of regret. The can doom you to: (p. 111)

a. _____

b. _____

c. _____

5. There are a number of "if only..." or "what if..." regrets that may apply to you. If so, choose from the ones listed on page 111, or you may have some that are uniquely yours. List them, confess them, and get rid of them forever!

6. We know we can't change the past, but what can we change? (p. 112)

7. The Lord has given us three powerful gifts to set us free from all of our regrets or "if onlys." What are these gifts that come from Him alone? (p. 112)

8. God's first remedy for the "if onlys" is grace: What is grace? (p. 112)

9. I believe that the reason so many of us feel miserable in life is because we have never _____

_____

_____

_____. (p. 112)

10. God's second remedy for the "if onlys" is mercy: What is mercy? (p. 112)

11. God says to us, "I'll intervene in your life with a miracle. I will have mercy on you when you don't even think I should or would! Because _____, I will _____ _____!" (p. 112)

12. God's third remedy: Grace and mercy are complemented by God's gift of _____ _____. What will God's peace guard for you? (pp. 112–113)

13. This message from my heart is for the Elect Lady. God interrupted your life to save it, but: (pp. 113)

a. until_____ _____,

b. His _____ _____,

c. His _____ _____.

Notes

14. What does God want us to do so that He can rescue us? (p. 113)

15. What happens to our lives when we find favor with God? (p. 113)

16. God can fix your "stuff" as long as _____ _____. Do you believe that is really true for your situation? Be honest with yourself.

17. God is speaking clearly to you today. He wants you to understand that He has great resolve in His heart to be there for you. Fill in the blanks of the following statement and then believe that this is the essence of His promise to you! (p. 113)

"Once and for all, Elect Lady whom I love (and this includes any children you may have), your _____

_____

so that I can put a little _____, _____,

and _____, if you can _____

_____

_____."

God is looking for people who will say, "I'm not going to fight you anymore, Lord." Listen, this isn't limited to just the Elect Ladies. There are some miserable men who have not accepted God's call or election. At an earlier time in my life, I was one of them.

I didn't *choose* to be a preacher. My daddy was a preacher, and the *last* thing I wanted to be was a preacher. I actually *ran* from it until God interrupted my life. I got fired from a dream job; I couldn't sleep at night; I was divorced and raising two boys as a single dad. God didn't give me any peace or grace in my situation until I finally accepted His election to be a pastor.

Even then I had to struggle with God's choice. Like many other young men in the ministry, I wanted to pastor an "important" church in Atlanta. But God had other plans for me. He called me to a small church in Cedartown, Georgia, that couldn't afford a full-time pastor. So I had to work a full-time job and make the 160 miles round-trip to the church each week, feeding my boys in the car as we traveled. It was not the dream of my heart, and I struggled with the Lord.

Finally, weeping and broken before God, I said, "Lord, I am going to pastor this church as if You've assigned me to these people for the rest of my life!" From that point on, I stopped looking for "something better" in Atlanta, and God's grace, mercy, and peace were mine. I moved to Cedartown and had a wonderful time in that congregation growing in numbers and in the Lord.

When the leadership of New Birth Missionary Baptist Church called me to come and be their pastor, it was one of the most agonizing decisions of my life. I had fallen in love with the people of Cedartown, and Atlanta was no longer the focus of my life. Plus, I didn't want to be *anywhere* that God didn't want me to be. When God made it clear that it was *His will* that I accept the new election to New Birth, His assurance was once again His *grace, mercy, and peace*!

18. Through these circumstances, I have learned that there are blessings when you are a man (or woman) under _____ from God, instead of a man (or woman) on _____. (p. 117)

19. In the circumstances of pastoring my first church, God gave me the grace, mercy, and peace to do it. What did I have to do first? (p. 117)

20. There are always uncertain times in our lives when we are unsure of the direction in which to go. Once you accept God's election in your life, it becomes an _____

_____

_____. (p. 118)

21. After many years, I have come to the place where I recognize and accept God's election in various parts of my life. I am *captivated and captured* by my investment in God's election! What about you? Write about your own election and how it has captivated you to serve the Lord.

22. Sometimes, when we follow our election, our motives can be questioned or criticized. When you know that your election is from the Lord, I encourage you to _____ _____ and to make your election speech _____ to all who will hear. (pp. 119–120)

THE Elect Lady WORKBOOK

Notes

_____
_____
_____
_____
_____
_____
_____
_____
_____
_____
_____
_____
_____
_____
_____
_____
_____
_____
_____
_____
_____
_____
_____
_____
_____
_____
_____
_____
_____
_____
_____
_____
_____

23. When we grab hold of what God really intends for us to do, we discover that it isn't _____, it's _____. It is God's purpose _____ _____. (pp. 120–121)

24. Mary lived out God's purpose, but so did her husband Joseph. The Bible never says that Mary convinced Joseph about the truth of her pregnancy. We are told that Joseph was _____ and accepted his own _____ with actions that amount to a loud "yes." Joseph's life was _____, too. (See Matthew 1:18–25) (pp. 121–122)

25. No one really likes to think about the price we may pay in our families and communities—or with our lives—for the election of God. Many of the biblical heroes paid a great price. What did they do, and what did it cost them? (p. 122)

a. *Isaiah* _____

_____

_____

_____.

b. *Jeremiah* _____

_____

_____

_____.

c. *Hosea* _____

_____

_____

_____.

26. Why might John the Baptist's father, Zacharias, been disappointed in his son? (p. 123)

27. Instead of being a disappointment, what was John the Baptist elected to do out of the entire human race? How did he handle his election? (p. 123)

28. After you accept your election and make your final election speech, what should you prepare for? (p. 125)

29. Paul told the Christians in Philippi to "_____

_____

_____" (Philippians 2:12).

God's gift of salvation is free. But once you are in God's

kingdom, He launches you on a process of maturity to

"_____" the _____

in your life. You will also be "_____"

the perfect will of God and the _____

_____

_____. (p. 125)

Notes

30. In another encouraging word, Colossians 1:27 speaks of *"Christ in you, the hope of glory."* What should we be doing with that living hope? (pp. 125–126)

31. Whatever God put in you before you were formed in your mother's womb is the _____ _____ to be worked out in you. (p. 126)

32. What is the "Eddie Long translation" of Philippians 2:13? (p. 126)

THOUGHTS FOR REFLECTION

Don't try to choose what has already been chosen! We create most of our own heartache because we run around in our own manmade enthusiasm and energy. We try to work out something in His name that He never ordained to be worked out of us. You can only give out of what has been deposited in you—and that is His will for your election.

Once you discover and accept your election in Christ, once you deliver your acceptance speech and step into your destiny, the awe of God will fall on your life. You will discover what it feels like to be fulfilled, because you will be doing what you were created to do, and nothing else will have that same appeal or satisfaction.

In your journal time, share your heart with the Lord concerning your election. If you don't know that call for certain, ask Him to reveal it to you. If you know your election, then write your acceptance speech to Him.

Notes

Reflections from the Heart

CHAPTER NINE

Silent Pondering, Public Suffering, Eternal Glory

To the Elect Lady... and Her Pondering Heart

"But Mary treasured up all these things, pondering them in her heart."
—Luke 2:19 (NASB)

The burden of a secret can seem unbearable at times. And no secret is so difficult to keep as a secret given by God.

Mary entered married life under the strangest set of circumstances ever faced by a woman on earth. She married Joseph in a "shotgun wedding" orchestrated by God. Then she had to live with Joseph almost as a friendly stranger for nine long months as they struggled to stand together as social outcasts in their society.

The day Mary said "yes" to God, He shared some secrets with her through the archangel. These were the "weighty" kind of secrets, divine mysteries that still baffle Jewish theologians to this day (because the key to these mysteries is the identity of Jesus as the Messiah of the Scriptures.)

Imagine a teenage Jewish girl hearing these words come from Gabriel, one of the two archangels who dwell in the very presence of God: *"Hail, favored one! The Lord is with you"* (Luke 1:28 NASB). Now begins Mary's *"pondering"* that will last a lifetime as she considers the One whom she was called to bring into this world.

Notes

UNDERSTANDING GOD'S ELECTION

1. Mary received many secrets from God to treasure in her heart. She learned from Gabriel that her cousin _____ had become _____ _____. (p. 130)

2. Describe what happened when Mary walked into Elizabeth's home for the first time. (pp. 130–131)

3. What other special name did Elizabeth give Mary after Elizabeth's baby had leapt for joy in her womb? (p. 131)

4. When the shepherds found Mary, Joseph, and Jesus in the stable, they said that angels visited them in the fields, saying, "*a* _____, *who is* _____ _____" (Luke 2:11 NASB) had been born in Bethlehem. (p. 131) How that young mother must have pondered such mysteries in her heart!

5. Have you pondered your own election from God? Have you asked Him what it all means? Write some of your thoughts down to the Lord right now. He is ready to hear your heart.

6. The elderly Simeon was a wise and righteous man in the temple who told Mary and Joseph the Father's destiny for Jesus, prophesying: (pp. 131–132)

Behold, this child is appointed _____

_____,

and for a sign to be opposed— _____

_____   _____

_____—to the end that thoughts from many hearts

may be revealed.   (Luke 2:34–35 NASB)

7. After twelve relatively "normal" years, Mary was jolted back into the reality of her divine election when Jesus stayed behind in Jerusalem after the Passover. What did Jesus say to His parents when they questioned His actions? (p. 132)

8. Mary was an Elect Lady, a woman set apart _____

_____,

whatever it might be. (p. 133)

9. How did Mary face the known and the unknown concerning her eldest and much-loved Son, and how must we face them as well? (p. 133)

Notes

10. The woman who carried the Seed of God and gave birth to our Savior also _____

_____

_____ all the days of her life. (p. 133)

I strongly suspect that most of God's Elect Ladies, and even his elect men, have received revelations that they must carry in their hearts and ponder all of their days.

It is time, dear sisters, to address those silent ponderings and quiet reflections that take up residence in our hearts after God speaks divine secrets to us—those things we can't talk about, that we wouldn't know how to share with other people. These are the things we must bring before the Lord in prayer and ponder all that they could possibly mean to us.

Most of us echo these words of Mary when we receive a genuine visitation from God: *"How can this be?"* (Luke 1:34 NASB). His ways really *are* higher than our ways, and His thoughts are infinitely greater than our thoughts and power of comprehension. (See Isaiah 55:9.)

11. Have you said to the Lord, "I hear Your words, but I can't understand Your ways?" Do you wonder how God will ever work out the details of your situation? Write down a situation that seems impossible to be accomplished without God's intervention.

12. Remember Mary's words to Gabriel, *"How can this be,*
_____ *?"* (Luke:1:34
NASB) Gabriel replied, *"The* _____ *will
come..."* (v. 35 NASB). (p. 134)

13. God's answer will *always* be the same, *"The Holy Spirit
will...!"* It is the Holy Spirit's presence and the power of
the _____ that will overshadow
us and accomplish everything we need in our life's
circumstances! (p. 134)

14. When God reveals secrets about His plans for our
lives, we often struggle to accept them. We begin to:
(p. 134)

a. evaluate _____,

b. seriously doubt_____

_____.

c. As a result, natural thinking _____

_____

_____.

15. Just like with David and Abraham, when the Lord
gives a word to you about your destiny, it will probably
come to you at your poorest moment. (p. 135) Can you
think of an example of this in your own life?

Notes

THE *Elect Lady* WORKBOOK

Notes

---

16. How do you deal with the unusual route of your destiny? Don't expect _____;
do expect _____

_____

_____. (p. 136)

17. We can always find comfort in God's Word, such as His promise in 1 Corinthians 10:12–13. We have looked at this Scripture before. This time, after you fill in these blanks, write it on a 3 x 5 card. Keep it close by you; memorize God's Word so that it will bring you comfort and strength during difficult days. (p. 136)

Therefore let him who thinks he stands take heed lest he fall. No temptation has overtaken you _____

_____*; and*

_____*, who will not*

allow you _____

_____*,*

but with the temptation _____

_____*, that you*

may be able to endure it. (1 Corinthians 10:12–13 NASB)

18. Sometimes our destinies in God are delayed for years, or even for a lifetime. How long was it between Simeon's prophecies to Mary and the pain of Jesus dying on the cross? (p. 136)

19. Thank God that the pain of the cross wasn't the end of Mary's destiny. She saw her Son as the risen Lord and Savior as told to her by the angel Gabriel. *Because God is faithful,* I am convinced that mothers

and grandmothers who pray for their children see the answers to their prayers in this _____ or over the _____ of _____! (p. 137)

20. What is the pattern that seems to occur for anyone elected by God for a special task? (p. 137)

21. Abraham and Sarah pondered the meaning of their covenant problem for _____.
They even attempted to_____
_____. (p. 137) (Please read Genesis 16.)

22. What did Abraham and Sarah's interference with God's plan trigger? (p. 137)

23. David must have pondered the meaning of why

_____
_____
_____. He didn't really understand _____
_____
_____. (p. 137–138) (Please read 1 Samuel 16, 19, and 20.)

THE *Elect Lady* WORKBOOK

Notes

24. Moses pondered God's words the first time the Lord spoke with him. What happened to Moses in that first encounter that would make anyone ponder? (p. 138)

25. Peter and the disciples pondered three and a half years of Jesus' teachings and actions. Peter in particular pondered Jesus' words at crucial times in his life: (p. 138)

a. the day Jesus called_____

_____

_____

_____;

b. the time Jesus praised _____

_____

_____

_____;

c. Jesus' final words spoken _____

_____

_____

_____;

d. the revelation by the Spirit _____

_____

_____

_____.

26. Mary of Bethany must have pondered the words of Jesus at Simon the leper's house. In Matthew 26:12–13 (NASB), what words do you think caused her to wonder the most? (pp. 138–139)

27. Saul the Pharisee was blinded by a white light and miraculously became Paul the disciple. Name two of the things that Paul pondered in his relationship as a servant of Jesus Christ. (p. 139)

28. The two men walking on the road to Emmaus must have pondered _____

_____

_____. Their words after Jesus vanished from their sight help us to understand what Spirit-inspired "pondering" really means: (p. 140)

They said to one another, "_____

_____

while He was speaking to us on the road, while He was

_____

_____?"   (Luke 24:32 NASB)

Notes

THOUGHTS FOR REFLECTION

Every Elect Lady has heard God whisper secrets to her heart if she stops long enough to listen. You may have heard someone say, "Abort that baby now; it's going to ruin your life." But God whispers to you, "This is *your* baby, protect and cover her with your life." The enemy says, "Why should you stick with this man? He ran around on you and mistreated you." The still small voice of God whispers, "You still love him and *I love him.* I put you two together so you could bring him home to Me." Friends and family may say, "Why should you take care of your daughter's, or your sister's kids? You have your own family to worry about." But a holy whisper blows across your heart, "This is what you were born for. They will live and become great tomorrow because *you are there for them* right now."

Once you hear the whisper of God, you can't turn away easily. Something in your heart just keeps burning. When you are about to give up, the voice of God echoes in your soul until you get up once again to face the new day.

Why? It is because you are *His Elect Lady.* What is on your pondering list today?

Reflections from the Heart

From One Elect Lady to Another

To the Elect Lady…
from First Lady Vanessa Long

"Behold the handmaid of the Lord; be it unto me according
to thy word."
—*Luke 1:38* (KJV)

(This chapter in *The Elect Lady* was written by First Lady Vanessa Long, wife of Bishop Eddie Long. It is from the heart of one Elect Lady to another.)

One of the most significant events in our ministry together took place the day my husband, Bishop Eddie Long, delivered the message "To the Elect Lady" for our annual women's conference. For me, it was as if God was saying directly to me, "I know you have some disappointments in your life. There were things that I know you wanted…and the life you have just doesn't match the picture you carried in your heart for so long. Your life has outgrown your early dreams but remember that *I haven't forgotten you.*"

My husband really touched a nerve in the women that morning. His strong word from the Lord met them right where they were—and that included me. When he read the first words of John's greeting, *"To the elect lady…"* before that packed house, something supernatural happened that surprised all of us. It was nothing less than a divine "setup" for transformation and visitation from the Lord. I would like to share through this study how I was personally touched by that message.

Notes

UNDERSTANDING GOD'S ELECTION

1. How can we know when a message such as this is the Lord speaking directly to us? It is when the _____ _____ puts His finger on the _____ _____ confronting us in this life. (p. 143)

2. What are many women confronted with today that threatens to steal any hope they have for a real future? (p. 143)

3. Because of what the Bishop saw in his own mother's life, the Lord has allowed him to be a tool to bring

_____.

(p. 144)

4. The message of the Elect Lady spoke to my heart personally, and I believe it continues to speak to the hearts of all women who are willing to listen. This is what the Lord wants to say to us: (p. 145)

I think you are special. You are an _____ _____, and you know I'm going to give _____, _____, and _____ to you. And I know where you are; _____ _____. You are special, and _____ _____!

I'm sharing what happened to me personally because sometimes it helps to know how other people cope with the pressures of life. In my circumstance, a lot of pressure naturally came my way from marrying a man who served the Lord in a high leadership position.

Eddie was the pastor of a growing church when we first met. I knew that the pastoral ministry could be demanding when we got married, but I wasn't ready for what was coming. Even though my husband is a wonderful pastor, I never expected the ministry to grow so large. I didn't realize Eddie would be this busy or that we would become a megachurch.

The success we enjoyed had its good points and its bad ones. I was happy to see the ministry bless so many people, and I was glad to see God use my husband in such a powerful way. At the same time, I began to notice that our children were missing their daddy. Many times, I had to hold things together alone. We knew we had to examine our priorities, regroup, reconnect, and put things back on the right road.

We had to really talk about the key problem areas— and we had to listen carefully to what the other one was saying. So we changed what we could change, and we adapted where we could adapt. We set apart one night a week as family night, and we had to put our family vacations "on the calendar" to make sure they happened. This crucial balancing act between priorities became just a normal part of our life, and we accept that now.

Yet, there are still sacrifices and commitments that we cannot avoid or lay aside without laying down God's call and election in our lives. Over the years I began to understand that "this election *is* our life." I began to realize that I had to truly trust God and to let go of my old dreams of daily "family time," of being like the television "Huxtable family" (produced and portrayed so well by Dr. Bill Cosby). Deep in my heart I knew, "This is the life God has given us, so this is the life we live. And we do it through His grace alone."

Notes

Whatever election God has called you to in this life, I encourage you to keep pressing forward. You can do it as we have—*through His precious grace alone.*

5. As Elect Ladies, God wants us to learn that *above all* we must _____ and _____ _____. (p. 150)

6. As he learned to trust God, what did the apostle Paul do? (See Philippians 3:14.) (p. 150)

7. What will happen if you place your life in God's hands? (pp. 150–151)

8. Have you ever felt that your circumstances meant that God did not love you? This is never true. But He may have something else that He wants to do with your life. (p. 151) Do you know someone whose dreams were completely redirected by the Lord?

9. We should never forget that it is not about *me and you*. Just who and what is this life all about? (p. 151)

10. God is giving me grace because my life today _____

_____

. (pp. 151–152)

11. If God has elected you to do the difficult and achieve the impossible, how should you walk out this call? What will your need to lean on God do for you? (p. 153)

12. A deeper relationship with God is the fruit of _____

_____. (p. 153)

Through all of the diligent search and struggle in my own life, God has enriched my relationship with Him. The Lord strengthened the weak areas in my life, and my husband and I realized more each day that God has placed us together so we could strengthen and challenge one another in our calling.

The morning Eddie delivered this message on "The Elect Lady" marked the beginning of a birthing process that helped me become the leader I am right now. It was a monumental moment in my life.

Notes

Once I accepted who I am and embraced the basic truths in this message, I felt a release from deep within my soul. God was telling me that it was okay to let my guard down and to let members of our church know that I face challenges in my life just like they do. I was tired of hiding behind a religious façade of perfection while pretending that everything is okay. God wanted people to see that I am a normal person who has to lean on Him *every day* just as they do. As Elect Ladies *together*, we can encourage one another to walk out the calling God has placed on each of our lives!

13. In the Bible, Mary is the woman whose story most inspires and encourages me as an Elect Lady. Her answer to the Lord has become my answer, and I hope your answer as well: "Let it be _____, _____, _____." (See Luke 1:38.) (p. 155)

14. Women are so relational that they can be hurt deeply through broken relationships. If you are still suffering from a broken relationship, write a prayer for the Lord's help in healing your heart, starting today.

My heart goes out to the millions of women who struggle to survive and preserve their lives and families. Think about the women you know who are single mothers, divorced women, women feeling trapped in difficult marriages, or women who have given up their dreams. Now make a list of their names. This is where your prayer life will take on a new dimension. Perhaps you and several other women you know can begin to pray for those who are hurting (even if *you* are one of them.)

Pray that the Lord would truly reveal Himself and the power of His election in their lives. Pray that His grace, mercy and peace would be poured out on them in abundant measure. Pray that they would have the strength—in whatever crisis they face—to say: "I will not continue to dwell on what I don't have. I will decide to go on and live!"

15. Everything moves forward or backward from this decision to move on with God or not. If you decide to focus on what you do *not* have, _____ _____. (p. 155)

16. If you choose to go on and live, how have you positioned yourself? (p. 156)

17. It all comes down to our _____ and our _____. Choose _____ and _____ the truth that God will bless you! (p. 156)

Notes

Notes

18. Again, what will happen if you continue to dwell on what you don't have? (p. 156)

19. There are some special groups of Elect Ladies who are close to my heart and remind me of some of the great women of faith in the Bible. God elects some ladies *to bear very special children under extremely difficult circumstances.* Name some women in the Bible who fall in this category. (p. 156, endnotes)

20. God's divine election always includes: (p. 156, endnotes)

a. _____ who face the difficult task of raising children alone,

b. _____ who spend their golden years _____

_____ ,

c. mothers and fathers who faithfully _____

_____ or care for

_____ .

21. There is a category of Elect Ladies who are called to marry and raise families with *men called to sacrificial ministries.* I would seem to fit in here. Can you think of

some other women that you know in this category? Write their names down now and add them to your growing prayer list.

22. In the Bible, women like Esther and Deborah were Elect Ladies who were called to _____

_____

_____. Deborah was actually a type of Old Testament *"mother in Israel"* and judge who, with Barak, helped to lead her nation to victory over its enemies. (p. 157, endnotes) Please read about Deborah's election in Judges 4 and 5, and write down some things that you see as special in her election to serve God.

THOUGHTS FOR REFLECTION

In each of these cases above, whether the women were from the Bible or live with us today, their choice was to accept their election and move on to all that God had for them. This same victory is available for you, dear sister. Choose life and believe the truth that God can bless you.

If you dwell on what you don't have, you truly will "dine" on past disappointments and offenses over and over again until you choose something else on the menu

Notes

of life. Once you put your trust in Him, you activate the key of faith to release all of the resources of heaven.

In the process, your life becomes a beacon of hope for everyone around you. Understand that God will use your life to encourage those around you and to let them know that He still loves them. Please consider this great love of God today.

Reflections from the Heart

CHAPTER ELEVEN

"Ain't God Good?"

To the Elect Lady...
and the Encouraging Word

"Therefore encourage one another and build each other up,
just as in fact you are doing."
—*1 Thessalonians 5:11* (NIV)

I know first-hand the power of the encouraging word. During the time I was preparing to go into the ministry in Richmond, Virginia, I went through a major crisis in ministry. The pastor at the church I was attending, Rev. Oly Brown, was a good man of God, and he befriended me.

I soon learned that Rev. Brown had another spiritual "asset" that would have an even greater impact on my life. This secret weapon was an elderly lady named Miss Beatrice Jones, who served as the pastor's housekeeper—and his prayer covering.

After the Reverend Brown passed away, God linked this wonderful woman's heart with mine, and she began to pray for me—literally, she "adopted me" in prayer.

We talked often over the years, (she is ninety-seven years old at the time of this writing) and she began every conversation basically the same way. She asked me some encouraging questions about my life and the growth of the ministry and then responded to my answers with the exclamation *"Ain't God good?!"*

Miss Jones always reminded me of the things she had seen happen in my life. No matter what problem I ever brought up, I could count on Miss Jones. No matter where we began, our conversations always ended with a focus on one truth above all others: *"Ain't God good?"* Every problem simply disappeared under the flood of praise she released to God. The encouragement of this precious woman, anointed by the Holy Spirit, literally made the difference between success and failure at key times in my life and ministry.

Never underestimate the power of an encouraging word!

UNDERSTANDING GOD'S ELECTION

1. What have men, women, and even the only-begotten Son of God benefited from? (p. 161)

2. I can't say it too often. In our Christian walk and through all of our trials, we must never underestimate

_____

_____! (p. 161)

3. True encouragers:

a. are people _____

_____;

b. they are _____;

c. their motives are _____

_____. (p. 161)

4. What is the primary difference between flattery and encouragement? (p. 161)

5. What two things qualify and equip special encouragers to properly relate to individuals and leaders? (p. 161)

Notes

6. In the Old Testament, the Hebrew word _____ is most often translated as *"encouragement."* (p. 162)

7. The word *chazaq* can mean "to fasten upon" as one possible definition. List three or four more definitions that fit this Hebrew word. (p. 162)

8. What was the most important topic that the Lord shared with Moses at the end of his long life? Why do you personally think that this was the topic God chose? (p. 162)

9. In Deuteronomy 3:28, God told Moses: (pp. 162–163)

Charge Joshua and _____

_____*; for*

he shall go across at the head of this people, and he shall

give them as an inheritance the land which you will see.

(Deuteronomy 3:28 NASB)

10. God knew it was important for Moses to deliver his word of encouragement to Joshua. Encouragement

would enable Joshua to be: _____, _____

_____, _____

_____, _____, _____, and

_____ so he could take hold and seize

God's Promised Land. (p. 163)

11. The Hebrew word *chazaq* appears many times in the book of Daniel. What two meanings does this word refer to in the Hebrew? (p. 163)

12. When Daniel saw the *"Angel of the Lord"* (who was probably Jesus Himself), he fainted, and even when revived, still trembled uncontrollably. What did the angel do to help Daniel stop trembling? (p. 163)

13. Encouraging words are vitally important in our walk with Christ. Let's look at the encouragement and strength that Daniel received from the Angel of the Lord. (pp. 163–164)

> *And he said, "O man of high esteem, do not be afraid.*
> *Peace be with you; take _____ [_____]*
> *and be _____ [_____]!" Now, as*
> *soon as he spoke to me, I received _____*
> *[_____] and said, "May my lord speak, for you*
> *have _____ [_____] me."*
>
> (Daniel 10:19 NASB)

14. Once again, in Daniel 10:21, the angel described the strength or *chazaq* of the Lord. (p. 164)

> *"Yet there is no one who* _____
> [_____] *with me against these forces except Michael your prince* [the archangel of God]."
>
> (Daniel 10:21 NASB)

15. Is there someone who gives you this *chazaq* in your life? Someone who stands firmly beside you, whose words bring you courage and strength? Name that person here and take the time to write a prayer of thanks to the Lord for sending you that special encourager.

16. In the New Testament gospels and epistles, we hear of the importance of the encouraging word. The Word of God is always our source _____. (p. 164)

17. In the book of Acts, Barnabas ministered with the apostle Paul. What did Barnabas' name mean? (p. 164)

18. In his letter to the Romans, Paul spoke of the

"_____

_____" (Romans 15:4 NASB). (p. 164)

19. What is Encouragement 101? (p. 164) Can you relate a specific time when God gave you a word of encouragement to help bring you through a time of stress or difficulty?

20. What are some of the ways that God *and* His people will encourage us when we feel overwhelmed and under-equipped? (p. 165)

21. Encouraging one another is what Paul was talking about in Philippians 2:1–4. After reading these verses, in your own words explain how the Lord wants us to be an encouragement to one another. (p. 165)

Notes

22. Elect Lady, you have a high calling to serve as a lifelong encourager to others. Using the list of people on page 165 and the circumstances in your own life, name some of the types of people you serve with encouragement.

23. The Lord gives us all the grace to do His will in life, but the Elect Ladies need _____

_____.

(pp. 165–166)

We all have Elect Ladies in our lives, but are we doing everything God calls us to do for them? The Elect Lady in my life, Vanessa, encourages me, and I couldn't fulfill my calling without her. But my encourager needs as much or more encouragement than I do.

What happens when God speaks to you at some "inconvenient time" about dropping your schedule and visiting the single mother who lives nearby? How many times have the men in our churches failed to recognize that it was God telling them about His Elect Ladies, admonishing them to play with those three boys who have no father, or teach the widow's sons how to become men. When will we hear the grandmothers who bombard heaven for someone to fix their roofs or floors so that their grandchildren will have a decent place to grow up?

24. The best answer in every situation is for each of us to
_____.
(p. 167)

25. God is very specific about His care for widows and orphans in several places in the Bible. What does He say about widows and orphans in James 1:27 (NASB)? (p. 167)

26. In Philippians 4:4–6, Paul has written what I like to refer to as "The Encourager's Anthem." What are some of the keys to this encouraging Scripture? (pp. 167–168)

a. Rejoice _____

b. Be anxious _____

c. With thanksgiving _____

_____.

27. In Philippians 4:8, Paul continues the encouragement. What types of things should occupy our thoughts?
(p. 168)

28. Just like my time with Miss Jones, when we encourage ourselves by lifting up praise to God, our days of gloom can be turned to _____. (p. 168)

Notes

THOUGHTS FOR REFLECTION

"Ain't God good?" Can we ever doubt Him? It was God—your God—who crafted and formed you in your mama's womb! It was God who first whispered your name into the universe, and it was that same God who gave you your *first* breath…who will be there with His scarred hand extended to lead you home when you take your *last* breath! *Ain't God good?* Of course He is!

Never underestimate the power of encouraging words! Receive them when they come, and be ready to give them to others at the slightest urging of the Holy Spirit. Ask for the gift mentioned by the prophet Isaiah, *"The Sovereign Lord has given me his words of wisdom, so that I know what to say* [how to encourage] *all these weary ones."* (Isaiah 50:4 NLT).

Reflections from the Heart

CHAPTER TWELVE

Preparing the Next
Generation of Elect Ones

To the Elect Lady…
Who Is a Sacrificial Nurturer

"Whoever loses his life for My sake, he is the one
who will save it."
—*Luke 9:24 (NASB)*

Sometimes you have to give up things you value to give birth to, or to nurture, things of even greater value. Ask any mother—especially a single mother—who must face her day-to-day tasks and the future alone. Ask any grandmother, aunt, or cousin who has sacrificed her personal freedoms and privileges to raise grandchildren, nephews, or nieces. Ask any adult child who has sacrificed things to care for an ill or incapacitated elderly parent.

Selfish people don't do a good job raising children or taking care of aged parents. They will bail out quickly or find ways to "dump" their responsibilities. When someone like Mary agrees to pay the price, her personal sacrifice for the sake of others touches countless lives in the generations to come. Your sacrifice will touch lives for Christ as well.

But we must ask ourselves some important questions as this study draws to a close. How do we help prepare the next generation of God's elect ones? Exactly how do we train young people to live sacrificially? What makes a young woman like Mary so willing to lay down her hopes and dreams for the sake of others?

Notes

UNDERSTANDING GOD'S ELECTION

1. The answer to training young people to live for the Lord begins and ends with God. (p. 171) In Philippians 2:13 (NASB) the Bible says,

> *"For _____ who is at work in you, both _____ and _____ for His good pleasure."*

2. We can also follow _____ _____ and learn the many ways He _____ _____ and a significant number of women for _____ _____! (p. 171)

3. What two motivations guided everything the Lord Jesus did? Which was His supreme motivation in all things? (p. 171)

4. What must we give the next generation to help them understand personal sacrifice?

5. Jesus used several things to train and teach the Twelve. He had methods and goals. Please list as many of them as you can find. (p. 172)

6. We must ask ourselves an important question: *Am I doing something worthy to pass on to others?* Feel free to write down the thing you believe God has called you to pass on to others.

7. Why is today's generation called "the entitlement generation?" What do they expect from jobs and life? (p. 173)

8. How do we help prepare this generation of young people who aren't used to sacrifice and diligence? (p. 174)

9. Jesus was quick to tell His disciples that once they agreed to follow Him, everything in life would go their way. (p. 174)

Circle one:

True or **False**

THE *Elect Lady* WORKBOOK

10. The apostle Paul described the way that He suffered for preaching the gospel and added, *"Indeed, all who desire to live godly in Christ Jesus _____*

_____" (2 Timothy 3:12 NASB). Jesus also said, *"Remember the word I said to you, 'A slave is not greater than his master.' If they persecuted Me, _____*

_____" (John 15:20 NASB). (p. 174)

Jesus did talk about persecution, but He did not say some of the things we say to people coming into the church to try to make it "easy" for them. He *did not* say: "If you really want to follow Me, just raise your hand while everyone's head is bowed—don't worry, nobody will see you." Jesus also *did not* say: "Now everything will be fine—you've got your lifetime pass to 'Jesus World'—just live like you want to live because My grace will cover you like grease in a skillet. I want you to be free to be you—*even if it makes you less like Me!* " And the Lord Jesus *never* said: "Never say 'no' to yourself; that might hurt your self-esteem!"

I'm sure you get the point: Jesus came to give us abundant life, but He never promised a life without difficulty or sacrifice.

11. Jesus did say something that many Christians overlook, ignore, or avoid most of their lives: (p. 175)

If anyone wishes to come after Me, _____

_____ and _____

_____, and follow Me. For whoever wishes to save his life _____, *but whoever* _____

_____ *, he is the one* _____

_____ .   (Luke 9:23–24 NASB)

12. Jesus trained and warned His disciples. What truths did He impart to them that we must share with the next generation? (p. 175)

13. If you really want to prepare young people to succeed in Christ, you have to teach them some basic things: (p. 175)

a. _____

b. _____

c. _____

_____

_____

14. Is your life a living book of instruction and training demonstrating the power of God to keep and preserve you in times of crisis? Have the young people around you seen you react in crisis as though God is in control? Explain.

Notes

Notes

15. The people God places in your life should be learning several key principles. While you list these principles below, think of the young people you know who could be helped by understanding them. (p. 176)

a. Life isn't _____

_____

_____

_____ .

b. God is _____

_____

_____

_____ .

c. Even the best humans _____

_____

_____ .

16. A heart like David's is a heart of _____ ,

that is focused on _____

_____ . (pp. 176–177)

17. What are some of the reasons why Elect Ladies have been pulled back from public ministry? (p. 177) Thank God for the power of the cross that enables us to return to ministry again!

18. Has a crisis or failure in your life pulled you out of active service for God? Explain.

19. In Matthew 6:31–33, God shows us how we can trade our viewpoint on material things for His viewpoint. Explain it from the Scripture in your own words. (p. 178)

20. In John 12:23–24, Jesus tells us how important it is that we *lose* ourselves to *find* ourselves. As you fill in these blanks, pray that the Lord will show you how this truth applies personally to you. (p. 178)

> *The truth is, a kernel of wheat must be planted in the*
> *soil.* _____
> _____ *—a single seed. But its death will* _____
> _____ *—a plentiful*
> *harvest of new lives. Those who love life in this world*
> _____ . *Those who despise their*
> *life in this world* _____
> _____ . (John 12:23–24 NLT)

21. The Bible is filled with powerful examples of people who invested time, energy and resources to prepare the next generation who were destined to be elected by God. As I stated earlier, Naomi and Ruth both _____
_____ . (p. 180)

Notes

22. Naomi covered Ruth and passed on spiritual life to her. Ruth married Boaz, and together they covered their son _____. Jesse produced _____ _____ for Ruth, and the youngest was _____. (p. 180)

23. What did God accomplish through King David? (p. 180)

24. Another example of mentorship is found in the book of Esther. Modecai covered his young cousin, Esther, protecting her even as she became Queen of Persia. What did Esther have to do to save her people? (p. 182)

25. The following Scripture concerning God's call and special timing reverberates through the heart of every Elect Lady, from Esther's time until today: (pp. 182–183)

Think not with thyself that thou shalt escape in the king's house, more than all the Jews. For if thou altogether

_____

_____, *then shall there enlargement and*

deliverance arise _____

_____; *but thou and thy father's*

house shall be destroyed: _____

_____

_____

_____? (Esther 4:13–14 KJV)

26. There are some lesser known Elect Ladies in the Scriptures who risked their lives to protect God's anointed. Jochebed is one of them. Who did she save, and how did she do it? What do we know that her son accomplished in biblical history? (pp. 183–184)

27. Hannah's passionate prayer influenced an empire. Remember, she was barren until she cried out to the Lord. God quickly answered her prayer and it was her son Samuel who _____

_____and paved _____

_____ .

(p. 184)

28. Solomon's mother, Bathsheba, accepted her election as one of God's Elect Ladies. What did she do for her son that was part of God's plan? (p. 185)

29. God used a little-known woman named Jehoshabeath to safeguard the line of King David. Her role was

important because she saved _____ _____who was

David's _____

_____ . (p. 185)

Notes

30. Jehoshabeath boldly snatched Joash from under his evil's grandmother's nose and hid him for six years. Once again the destiny _____

_____

_____, waiting for an Elect Lady who would risk her life to preserve God's chosen leader. (p. 186)

31. Take courage, dear sister. God still uses _____

_____

_____! (p. 186)

32. Now that you have looked into God's heart and His Word concerning the Elect Lady, how would you describe your election today? Do you see it more clearly that ever before? Share your heart with the Lord today.

THOUGHTS FOR REFLECTION

Elect Lady, now that you have done this study, I believe that you understand more clearly that ever before God's attitude toward you. *You are special and precious in His sight!* There is something holy about people (women and men) who willingly lay down their lives—their dreams, goals, and desires—to help others. It reminds me of Someone very special who left His throne and heavenly crown behind to set all of mankind free by laying down His own life for others.

Be encouraged. This promise from God's Word truly applies to you today:

*God is not unjust; **he will not forget** your work and the love you have shown him as you helped his people and continue to help them.*

(Hebrews 6:10 NIV, emphasis added)

You are in good company. Keep the faith. Keep your eyes on Jesus. Never give up! Surround yourself with God's Word and His believing people. The Lord's next generation of worshippers and leaders is depending on you!

Answer Key

CHAPTER ONE
To the Elect Lady...

1. His own plans and purposes; perform kingdom pursuits

2. God has chosen the foolish things of the world, the base things of the world, that no flesh should glory in His presence.

3. His wisdom; divine plan; human qualifications or abilities

4. Answers will vary.

5. possess God's blessing; forfeit the blessing

6. Answers will vary.

7. Answers will vary.

8. These words offer the hope of healing and divine purpose to everyone burdened by questions of "what might have been." These words can release us from the memories that replay in our minds.

9. broken places inhabited by lost opportunities; disappointed expectations; buried remnants of past betrayals

10. Answers will vary.

11. destiny; chooses us

12. the plans I have for you; for good; for disaster; future; hope

13. your holy destiny; These plans are meant to give me a future and a hope!

14. He had elected (chosen) John to cover His mother for the rest of her life on earth. He also made it clear that Mary was to cover John for his life as his mother.

15. Answers will vary.

16. will never let you down; be pushed past your limit; help you come through it

17. Answers will vary.

18. could not; would not; Answers will vary.

19. deepest joy; greatest power

20. Answers may vary some by Bible translations. 1) Let us therefore come boldly to the throne of grace, that we may obtain mercy and find grace to help in time of need. 2) Be my strong habitation, to which I may resort continually; You have given the commandment to save me, for you are my rock and my fortress. 3) Therefore do not be like them. For your Father knows the things you have need of before you ask Him.

21. Answers will vary.

22. Elect Lady; the American Dream; the things of God

23. God is making them a catalyst that will speed them into their destinies.

24. yielded; accepted

25. Answers will vary but may include: True manhood is at a lower level today. Women try to escape their homes early.

26. "bought with a price"

27. seek God's plan for their lives; to God's Word; first

28. from your childhood dreams

29. to go after their dreams; to achieve great things; to accomplish whatever they put their minds to

30. God gives me the grace to do whatever I put my mind to do.

CHAPTER TWO
"If You Leave Me, I Will Die"
To the Elect Lady... Who Is Our Hero

1. for me to extend spiritual fatherhood to countless people and entire church congregations around the world today

2. Answers will vary.

3. Answers will vary.

4. steadfast in selfless love; the love of Jesus

5. to cover the precious ones God had placed in her womb and in her life

6. Answers will vary.

7. we must never forget the price they paid on our behalf; as much as possible, we should be there for them when they need us in later years.

8. Answers will vary.

9. Answers will vary.

10. rise up and call her blessed; also, and he praises her

11. forgive them, for they do not know what they do

12. He exercised tender care for His mother. He took care of the Elect Lady in His life.

13. "Dear woman, here is your son." "Here is your mother." took her into his home

14. Answers will vary.

15. pray for them

16. Answers will vary.

17. Answers will vary.

18. fought the good fight; finished the race; kept the faith; the crown of righteousness

19. Blessed. Other answers will vary.

20. Examples could include Esther, Hannah, Ruth. Other answers will vary.

CHAPTER THREE

Arrested and Interrupted by Destiny

To the Elect Lady... Whose Plans Have Been Disrupted

1. outward circumstances; presence; absence

2. are not your thoughts, neither are your ways my ways, saith the Lord. For as the heavens are higher than the earth, so are my ways higher than your ways and my thoughts than your thoughts

3. The foolish plan of God is far wiser than the wisest of human plans.

4. Modern society tends to wink at unwed mothers. In Mary's day, her pregnancy would have been a total disgrace.

5. through the miraculous action of the Holy Spirit

6. to do His will; at risk of rejection; arrest and intervene; begin blessing and covering her

7. Answers will vary.

8. God's will is done through one obedience, one sacrifice, and one step of faith at a time.

9. Answers will vary but may include: backbiting, gossip, disgrace, women refusing to let their daughters speak to Mary.

10. Mary felt the pain of social rejection and misunderstanding; the pain of childbirth; the searing pain of her soul when Jesus was crucified.

11. God was bringing about the birth of a far greater thing

12. "This child is destined for the rise and fall of many in Israel."

13. A sword will pierce through Mary's soul because of Jesus' destiny.

14. Answers will vary.

15. False. Only God can truly choose the best for us.

16. when God called you; God deliberately chose things; He chose those; God chose things; ever boast in the presence of God

17. producing a lifetime of regret

18. a season of divine rearrangement; a divine adjustment; realigning your life

19. He elected me because He loves me.

20. He will not let me be tempted beyond what I can bear.

21. The real challenge of trust is when my faith must cover several years without seeing any progress in the direction of my dreams.

22. way of the world; easy counsel of their unsaved friends

23. a divine plan for that little one's life

24. We have all sinned, and we all need the cleansing blood of Jesus to wash away our sin.

25. it to the Lord; to forgive you; His mercy and grace; give you a new start in life

26. If we sin, Jesus Christ will plead for us before the Father. He takes away our sin and the sin of the world.

27. Yes; you have confessed your sins; reach someone else

28. He reacted with kindness. He offered her the living water of life. She became a great evangelist, telling others what Christ had done for her.

29. to be champions for Christ; for the cross; for a drug deal; a missionary assignment; into that place of darkness and despair

30. He will turn my pain and sorrow into fuel to feed the fire of His anointing.

CHAPTER FOUR

"I Don't Remember the Last Time I Woke Up Happy"

To the Elect Lady... Who Needs Joy

1. blessed dream of God

2. Answers will vary.

3. had a plan and the power to fulfill His vision

4. It took obedience. He led them step-by-step.

5. David's situation seemed lowly because he was the youngest son; he was out in the wilderness; he was a shepherd; he was never called in for special occasions like his brothers.

6. God's carefully crafted dream

7. his wife; his home; his position of honor; his opportunity to worship before the Ark

8. He pressed deeper into God's presence through prayer, praise and worship.

9. Fill out a note card with Psalm 40:1–3.

10. Answers will vary.

11. husband; two sons; their husbands

12. Answers will vary.

13. She had been totally transformed from a Moabite woman to a devoted daughter and a servant of Naomi's God by faith.

14. Entreat me not to leave you; for wherever you go, I will go; shall be my people; your God, my God.

15. God directed their steps to Boaz who married Ruth. Boaz provided for Naomi and Ruth, and gave Ruth a son who became the father of King David and placed them in the lineage of Jesus Christ.

16. thinking; relationship; life situation

17. We need to partner with Him through obedience.

18. Answers will vary.

19. ability to trust God with our lives

20. steal away every word from God that you have ever heard

21. the devil; lest they should believe and be saved

22. He uses cares, riches, and the pleasures of life.

23. that they may have life, and that they may have it more abundantly

24. the written Word (the Bible); the prophetic word; the inward word

25. noble and good heart; honest and full of good things

26. seize it, hold it down, protect it, treasure it, and conceal it inside our heart

27. Our goal should be to bear good fruit. We accomplish these things with patience.

28. you cooperate with Him in faith and don't give up

CHAPTER FIVE

Search for Significance in Your Crisis (Never Make It Your Home)

To the Elect Lady... Who Is Searching for Meaning

1. the preacher hears God all the time

2. hear or recognize His voice very well

3. saved murderers, saved adulterers, saved drug addicts, saved gangsters, even saved seminary students

4. We can make a difference with Christ working in us.

5. They are looking for something to live for, a burning purpose of significance.

6. pretend lives

7. mission and purpose

8. Answers will vary.

9. purpose and destiny in pursuit of God; filled with meaningless motion and energy expenditure; from God's direction and power

10. Answers will vary.

11. God causes all things to work together for good; called according to His purpose

12. cause them to work together for our good

13. He compared it to the valley of the shadow of death.

14. green pastures; still waters; restored souls; paths of righteousness

15. We set up our tents in the midst of our sorrows.

16. She was barren. She turned to the Lord in fervent prayer.

17. Answers will vary.

18. resigned to our crisis

19. He called us to be the head and not the tail.

20. False. He gives us the ability to turn our circumstances around.

21. He came to bring abundant life.

22. her problem to the One who is able to transform any situation; her heart's desire with God and promised it to Him

23. Jesus; absolute power and authority; set you free; brand new life

24. Answers will vary.

25. He will reveal the significance of my crisis and show me how to come out of it.

26. to preach the gospel to the poor; to heal the brokenhearted; proclaim liberty to the captives; of sight to the blind; at liberty those who are oppressed

27. unacceptable

28. I should stand up and call upon God's name. He will intervene on my behalf.

CHAPTER SIX

Don't Get Stuck in Transition

To the Elect Lady... Who Is Caught Up in the Process

1. Answers will vary.

2. Answers will vary.

3. We waste time and precious energy.

4. up; not down

5. Our focus should be on what is still there, not on what is gone.

6. of the vision of God; life-changing transformation; thinking; spirit; you live

7. giving my life to raise them—no matter what happens in this life

8. Answers will vary.

9. The timing of things can be very discouraging.

10. all of their dreams; achieve what they want in life

11. struggle for others

12. Answers will vary.

13. They can push us into a "garden of Gethsemane" experience.

14. crushing, lonely place; of painful rejection; misunderstanding; brokenness

15. Answers will vary.

16. confirmation; affirmation; the destiny planted in us

17. "Why are you staying in that marriage? He's just a jerk and you know it."

 "Can't you just leave the children somewhere else, like with a family member someplace?"

18. and let life choose for them; making choices based on the understanding

19. Answers will vary.

20. It is a joy that supplies strength, endurance and focus to take you through everything that comes along.

21. who for the joy set before Him endured the cross, despising the shame

22. 1) surrender; follow 2) accept; impossible task.

23. peace that surpasses and understanding and comprehension; guard your mind and protect your heart all the way through

24. yes; God's election; the cross to the grave; resurrection

25. I may have a divine appointment to help others who have broken dreams.

26. isn't your own; bought with a price; to live for Jesus; freedom to others

27. The only proper way to perceive God's will is to see your destiny and what you were elected to do from the position of God's high place.

28. Answers may vary but should include: mandatory retirements, raising grandchildren; weary caregivers.

CHAPTER SEVEN

How to Keep Going after Saying "Yes"
To the Elect Lady... Who Has Agreed to God's Plan

1. Our habit of camping around yesterday's ways is a serious challenge. "Oh, that's how we've always done it."

2. the kingdom of God

3. Three eternal truths are the cross, the blood, and the principles of new covenant life.

4. Answers will vary.

5. He empowered us to rule His creation together.

6. God created men and women to be equal in essence and different in function.

7. cover her children; self-sacrifice; faithful love

8. unless it abides in the vine; unless you abide in Me; he bears much fruit; you can do nothing

9. All of God's resources, with all of His grace and mercy, become available to you from that point on.

10. into alignment with God's purpose for us

11. He has deposited heavenly treasure in us. It will enable us to fulfill His good purpose for us as we yield to Him.

12. Answers will vary.

13. rejected by His own; empowered Him to perceive and seize the joy awaiting Him when all things were complete

14. grace; mercy; peace

15. salvation, hope and a future

16. Peace means God's stability in the midst of any and every storm we encounter in life. It does not mean the absence of trouble.

17. about Jesus; about Jesus; Answers will vary.

18. "Peace, be still!"

19. Jesus simply told the chaos to stop and peace to reign. The peace of God is perpetual and continuous.

20. see the way He has created to get us out of the situation

21. Answers will vary.

22. but I don't do it; the very thing I hate; I want to do right; Jesus Christ our Lord; no condemnation for those who belong to Christ Jesus

23. obedience; learning, adjustment; humility

24. in the middle of a raging storm; He really is; with you in every situation; sink or drown

25. The Lord promises to keep me in peace if I will keep my focus and attention on Him rather than on all the cares of life.

26. such as is common to man; God is faithful; not allow; will provide the way of escape also; to endure it

27. Answers will vary.

28. The election of God usually pulls you out of the crowd.

29. the yoke of our slave mentality; divine freedom in Christ

30. say "no" to how you used to think; to live in true freedom; for Him is your guide

31. For Christ, Paul gave up his education, his reputation, his Pharisaic commission and his very life.

32. deny himself and take up his cross

CHAPTER EIGHT

Don't Reject Your Election

To the Elect Lady... and Her Acceptance Speech

1. Answers will vary.

2. The "I/O Factor" is saying "If only," and living in regrets.

3. It will rob your destiny and destroy your dreams.

4. a hopeless future of backward thinking; endless stormy waves of remorse; rising winds of bitterness

5. Answers will vary.

6. We can change our present and affect our future.

7. grace, mercy and peace

8. Grace is kindness or favor given when we do not deserve it.

9. accepted the grace of God's forgiveness and His election

10. Mercy is when God helps us in a miserable situation, whether it was caused by disobedience or by something unrelated to a failure on our part.

11. I love you; step into your miserable situation and have mercy on you.

12. supernatural peace; God's peace will guard my heart and my mind.

13. you accept what you were called to be and do; grace and mercy will elude you; supernatural peace will be hard to find.

14. We must come to Him and find our place in His plans to receive His blessings.

15. When you find favor with God, people just have to bless you. Every time you turn around, God is blessing you.

16. you are obedient; Answers will vary.

17. life has been interrupted; mercy; favor; peace in it; accept what I elected you to do

18. assignment; the hunt

19. First, I had to prove myself faithful to His election in my life.

20. anchor of stability in times of instability

21. Answers will vary.

22. accept your election; loud and clear

23. a job; a joy; lived out in the flesh

24. obedient; election; interrupted by God

25. Isaiah accepted his election to prophesy the coming of the Savior and the end times. He was sawn in half. Jeremiah was a social outcast whose true prophecies and dire warnings were unheeded by the people. Hosea was instructed to marry an adulterous wife as an analogy of the Israelites unfaithfulness toward God.

26. Instead of following Zacharias into the priesthood, John the Baptist lived in the desert wearing camel skins and dunking people in the muddy water.

27. John the Baptist was elected to prepare the way of the Lord. He handled his election with excellence.

28. Prepare for an exciting and sometimes stretching ride with destiny.

29. work out [their] own salvation with fear and trembling; work out; imperfections; working out; election that He planted deep within you

30. We should be bringing that hope forth into our everyday life.

31. divine destiny He ordained

32. The Spirit of Christ is at work in you, providing the willpower and the real power to do His good pleasure.

CHAPTER NINE
Silent Pondering, Public Suffering, Eternal Glory
To the Elect Lady... and Her Pondering Heart

1. Elizabeth; pregnant in her old age

2. Elizabeth grabbed her stomach and called Mary blessed among women.

3. the mother of my Lord

4. Savior; Christ the Lord

5. Answers will vary.

6. for the fall and rise of many in Israel; and a sword will pierce even your own soul

7. "Why is it that you were looking for Me? Did you not know that I had to be in My Father's house?"

8. to embrace the will of God

9. We face them by relying upon the Unchanging One, by leaning upon God's faithfulness.

10. carried a burden in her soul that remained with her

11. Answers will vary.

12. since I am a virgin; Holy Spirit

13. Most High

14. our worth; that we are worthy to walk in what we heard; can easily lead us into disobedience rooted in unbelief

15. Answers will vary.

16. a straight route; to find obstacles blocking your way from time to time

17. but such as is common to man; God is faithful; to be tempted beyond what you are able; will provide the way of escape also

18. It was thirty-three years.

19. life; banisters; heaven

20. The pattern is the delivery of divine revelation followed by seasons of silent pondering and private and public suffering.

21. twenty-five years; "help" God in their frustration

22. Their interference created centuries of interfamily rivalry between the descendants of Ishmael and Isaac.

23. Samuel anointed him right in front of his father and brothers; his destiny as Israel's future king

24. God spoke to Moses from a burning bush and told him to speak to Pharaoh in spite of Moses' weaknesses.

25. him to come out of the boat and step on the water by faith; Peter for seeing His true identity and moments later said "Get behind me, Satan"; after Peter's betrayal and the Lord's resurrection, "Do you love Me?" and "Feed My sheep"; that God had included the non-Jewish world in His invitation to eternal life through Christ.

26. "Wherever this gospel is preached in the whole world, what this woman has done will be spoken of in memory of her."

27. While he was blind, Paul wondered what would happen to him after Jesus told him to enter the city. He pondered the divine revelations he received during visions of the "third heaven."

28. the words of the freshly resurrected Christ for the rest of their lives; Were not our hearts burning within us; explaining the Scriptures to us

CHAPTER TEN

From One Elect Lady to Another

To the Elect Lady... from First Lady Vanessa Long

1. Holy Spirit; pulse of the problems

2. Many women are confronted with disappointment, betrayal, delays and aborted dreams.

3. comfort, healing, and direction

4. Elect Lady; grace, mercy, peace; I haven't forgotten about you. I'm using you for My glory!

5. trust in God; never give up

6. Forget what lies behind; press on toward the goal of the upward call in Christ Jesus.

7. Even if your dreams aren't realized, God will replace your dreams with His.

8. Answers will vary.

9. It's all about Jesus and drawing others to His love.

10. is part of my election in Christ

11. I should walk out this call on my knees in prayer. If I lean on God, it will deepen and enrich my relationship with Him.

12. an honest heart cry to God

13. unto me, Lord, according to Your will

14. Answers will vary.

15. you automatically forfeit your future

16. I have positioned myself to reclaim my future.

17. attitude; faith; life; believe

18. I will "dine" on past disappointments and offenses until I choose something else on the menu of life.

19. Answers may vary but can include: Mary, Sarah, Rachel, Ruth, Hannah

20. single mothers; grandmothers; raising their grandchildren; raise special needs children; aged parents

21. Answers will vary.

22. sacrificial leadership functions in the kingdom; Answers will vary.

CHAPTER ELEVEN

"Ain't God Good?"

To the Elect Lady... and the Encouraging Word

1. They have benefited from the power of encouragement and the encouraging word.

2. the power of an encouraging word

3. who keep their spirits clean; above reproach; pure without doubt

4. The primary difference is purity of heart.

5. Purity of spirit and the absence of private agendas qualify us.

6. "chazaq"

7. to be courageous; to strengthen; to bind, restrain, conquer; other answers will vary.

8. The most important topic was encouragement. Answers will vary.

9. encourage him and strengthen him

10. constant; courageous; hardened (for battle); mighty; stout; strong

11. This word refers to encouragement and strengthening.

12. The angel spoke an encouraging word.

13. courage [*chazaq*]; courageous [*chazaq*]; strength [*chazaq*]; strengthened [*chazaq*]

14. stands firmly [*chazaq*]

15. Answers will vary.

16. of strength

17. Son of Encouragement

18. encouragement of the Scriptures

19. Encouragement 101 is God's Word and our personal strength class. Answers will vary.

20. God's presence will enfold us like a blanket of strength and encouragement. People will encourage us with a brotherly hug, an encouraging word, or a prophetic exhortation.

21. Answers may vary but should include: the Lord wants us to encourage one another with love and fellowship in His Holy Spirit, to show affection and compassion, to be humble to one another.

22. Answers will vary.

23. a special measure of mercy and grace just to survive

24. obey God's voice

25. It is pure and undefiled religion in the sight of God to visit them in their distress.

26. in the Lord always; for nothing; let your request be made known to God

27. We should think on whatever is true, honorable, right, pure, lovely, of good repute, excellent, worthy of praise.

28. total victory

CHAPTER TWELVE

Preparing the Next Generation of Elect Ones
To the Elect Lady... Who Is a Sacrificial Nurturer

1. it is God; to will; to work

2. in the footsteps of Jesus; prepared twelve men; a take over of the world systems

3. He was obedient to His Father in all things. He loved us. Love

4. We must give the next generation real-time, hands-on, up-close and personal demonstrations of what it means to die to self for the good of others.

5. Jesus spent time with the disciples in fields, synagogues, the temple, crowds. He used everyday events, real ministry assignments, and difficult obstacles. He equipped them to follow in His footsteps.

6. Answers will vary.

7. They expect success, good jobs, good wages and benefits, and the privileges of power from the beginning.

8. Like Jesus, we always tell them the truth.

9. False. Jesus spoke of suffering for the gospel.

10. will be persecuted; they will also persecute you

11. let him deny himself; take up his cross daily; shall lose it; loses his life for My sake; who will save it

12. That we must be filled with eternal hope, but still live by faith, that hard times will come.

13. Hear God's voice for themselves; Fall in love with Him; Honor His Word above every human opinion or conclusion.

14. Answers will vary.

15. (a) a movie, and sometimes you won't be rescued by the proverbial knight in shining armor;

(b) good and He will honor every promise He has made to you, but you will be hurt by other people in life; (c) among us fail to measure up to His standards

16. repentance; pleasing God more than man

17. Some of the reasons are family circumstances, unplanned pregnancies as unwed mothers, economic failures and even criminal activity.

18. Answers will vary.

19. Instead of seeking food, drink, and clothing, we should seek God and His kingdom first. He will take care of all of the rest.

20. Unless it dies it will be alone; produce many new kernels; will lose it; will keep it for eternal life

21. accepted their election

22. Jesse; eight grandsons; David

23. Through King David, God transformed the history of Israel and Judah and ushered in the coming of His Son, Jesus Christ.

24. Esther had to risk her life.

25. holdest thy peace at this time; to the Jews from another place; and who knoweth whether thou art come to the kingdom for such a time as this

26. Jochebed saved Moses. She hid him from Pharaoh in the basket on the Nile River. He was used by God to set the Hebrews free.

27. brought reform to Israel; the way for David to ascend to the throne

28. Bathsheba told David that there was a plot to overtake his throne by Prince Adonijah. Bathsheba's son Solomon was then crowned king instead.

29. Joash; only living male descendant

30. of a nation and the fulfillment of divine prophecy hung in the balance

31. His Elect Ladies to preserve His seed in our nation and around the world

32. Answers will vary.

Reflections from the Heart

Reflections from the Heart

About the Author

 ddic L. Long is the visionary and leader for New Birth Missionary Baptist Church. Since his installation in 1987, New Birth's membership has quickly multiplied from 300 to well over 25,000. In that time, Bishop Long directed numerous building expansions, land acquisitions, and building development efforts. These efforts led to the construction of a 3,700-seat sanctuary in 1991, a Family Life Center in 1999, and a 10,000-seat complex in 2001. He also serves as the founder and CEO of Faith Academy, New Birth's school of excellence. Located in the heart of DeKalb County, Georgia, in the city of Lithonia, New Birth Missionary Baptist Church continues to impact the community through countless outreach programs and community-empowering projects.

A native of North Carolina, Long received his bachelor's degree in business administration from North Carolina Central University and a master's of divinity degree from Atlanta's Interdenominational Theological Center. Additionally, Long has received honorary doctorates from North Carolina Central University, Beulah Heights Bible College of Atlanta, and the Morehouse School of Religion.

Bishop Long is revered locally, nationally, and internationally as a dynamic man of vision, leadership, integrity, and compassion. He serves on an array of boards, including the Morehouse School of Religion Board of Directors, the Board of Visitors for Emory University, the Board of Trustees for North Carolina Central University, the Board of Trustees for Young Life, the Board of Trustees for Fort Valley State University, the Board of Directors for Safehouse Outreach Ministries, and the Board of Trustees for Beulah Heights Bible College. He is also an honorary member of the 100 Black Men of America. Bishop Long has been named one of America's 125 most influential leaders and has received a plethora of awards in recognition of his world-changing ministry. In 2004, Bishop Long established a mentorship program known as the Longfellows Summer Academy to assist in the mental, physical, and spiritual development of young men between the ages of twelve and sixteen. What began as an eight-week program quickly developed into a lifelong commitment. And with this new commitment, Bishop Long began to raise funds earmarked for educational scholarships for the sixty-three charter members of the Long-fellow Summer Academy.

Bishop Long's *Taking Authority* broadcast, which is seen in 170 countries worldwide, has received more than 40 nationally recognized honors. A noted author, Bishop Long's captivating and powerful messages are masterfully captured in a number of books, as well as audio and video series, including *I Don't Want Delilah, I Need You; The Spirit of Negativity and Familiarity and Kingdom Relationship; Power of a Wise Woman; What a Man Wants, What a Woman Needs; Called to Conquer; Gladiator: The Strength of a Man; Taking Over,* and his most recent, *It's Your Time.*

Bishop Long and his wife, Vanessa, are the proud parents of four children: Eric, Edward, Jared, and Taylor. The couple has also served as surrogate parents for many other children in the church and community.

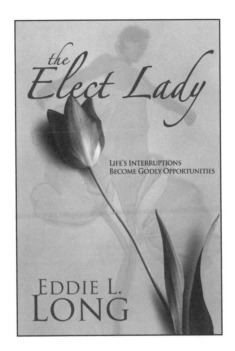

The Elect Lady:
Life's Interruptions Become Godly Opportunities
Eddie L. Long

Growing up, every little girl dreams of loving husbands, beautiful homes, and perfect children. What happens when life doesn't turn out the way she expected?

To all the women who wonder what went wrong in their lives, Bishop Eddie Long brings this powerful message. The path God has called you to may not be easy, but you are in the position to influence your children, your neighborhood, your church, and the world. *The Elect Lady* will cause you to claim God's best for your life, turn past mistakes into triumphs, and recognize God's interruptions in your life as divine direction. God has a better plan for you than you can imagine for yourself. Discover it today!

ISBN: 978-0-88368-281-4 • Hardcover • 192 pages

www.whitakerhouse.com

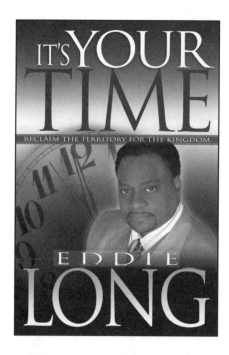

It's Your Time:
Reclaim Your Territory for the Kingdom
Eddie L. Long

Have we, as believers, allowed the world to silence us?

By slowly eroding our rights to free speech…
by passing laws saying that marriage isn't necessarily
between a man and a woman…
that murder is okay…
that it's wrong to display the Ten Commandments…
Is this really equality for all, except for Christians?

Join Eddie Long in reclaiming what has been lost. He will inspire you to rise up, take authority, and boldly assert your power as a believer. Discover how to redefine your life's purpose and vision while you raise your children to be godly leaders. Speak up, Christians! Now is the time for our unified voice to be heard, to take a stand together, and to stand firm. It's our time.

ISBN: 978-0-88368-783-3 • Hardcover • 192 pages

WHITAKER
HOUSE

www.whitakerhouse.com